RTÉ

N THE POORER QUARTERS

Aidan Mathews

VERITAS

First published 2007 by
Veritas Publications
7/8 Lower Abbey Street
Dublin 1
Ireland
Email publications@veritas.ie
Website www.veritas.ie

ISBN 978 1 84730 027 0

A catalogue record for this book is available from the British Library.

Printed in the Republic of Ireland by Betaprint Ltd, Dublin

Veritas books are printed on paper made from the wood pulp of managed forests. For every tree felled, at least one tree is planted, thereby renewing natural resources.

CONTENTS

For Lorelei Harris
From jewgreek to greekjew

INTRODUCTION

NOTHING IN THIS LITTLE BOOK is in any way original. For a would-be writer whose culture acclaims the tedium of individuality as the supreme prize in life and prosecutes plagiarism as the most despicable action of an author, the joy of the Judeo-Christian scriptures consists precisely in the opposite experience; that's to say, in the dear communion of the living and the dead who have been telling and retelling the stories of the Hebrew Bible and the Christian scriptures down the companionable millennia. Yet the Good News is always new notwithstanding and if any one person has shown this to be the case in our own time, it is surely the French anthropologist/theologian René Girard in whose Californian classroom, when I was young enough to be my own son, I heard a new teaching and with authority. It changed my life when I was auburn and it has gone on living my changes now that I am ash. The trees that were stripped to make these printed pages will not altogether resent my pretensions if their readers move from my jottings to his magisterial works on violence, religion and the nature of culture which furnish a completely convincing contemporary interpretation of the Passion narratives in the New Testament. Go, google.

If the commentary is not original, neither are the personal details. Anyone who has reached late middle-age has kept the same appointments and disappointments as I have. It is the commonality of such venues that makes them peculiar. But I do have a particular affinity with those individuals who have had to learn to be patients in an impatient world. Even as a child, I wanted to speak out on behalf of victims; but I never for a moment wanted to be one, least of all a manic depressive who would do damage to himself and to those around him. Mental illness meant otherwise. Unlike the woman in the gospel who cannot stop menstruating and is therefore always and everywhere unclean, soggy and stinking (she is the type of our affliction), I have never touched the hem of the garment of Jesus of Nazareth who healed, they say, with his own spittle and mud; but I have been touched by much considered kindness that was cut from the very same cloth, and for thirty years now I have been going in and out of a place of sanity which is the mutable body of my bride, a sweetheart with stretchmarks. These are not the things to say when one is preparing a preface to meet the prefaces that one meets, but it was she who showed me that a desolate state can be a modest apostolate, as Colossians somewhere suggests, if mischief seasons wistfulness. So, to her and to those who have walked the carpetless corridors in the night world of nicotine and lithium, greetings, good wishes, grace to you all. Well or ill, even or odd, visitant or visited, our roused, arisen Lord does indeed be with us.

Aidan Mathews
Lent 2007

In the Poorer Quarters *is a collection of Aidan Mathews' scripts from the programme of the same name broadcast on RTÉ Radio One from December 2005 to December 2006.*

Chapter One
CHRIST'S MASS

I WAS WORKING as part of the radio team on the broadcast of the Midnight Mass (Luke 2:1-20) on Christmas Eve in the Jesuit church in Gardiner Street, Dublin. My dad used to bring me to confession there in the 1960s, when women wore headscarves to protect their hairstyles from the wind and men wore bicycle-clips to protect their trousers from the chain. That was before the present structure of the sacrament of penance died a death because it had ceased to be useful to the community it was intended to serve (the rite of reconciliation, after all, is made for man and not man for the rite of reconciliation). I imagine my father chose Gardiner Street instead of the transept in his own parish out of subliminal spiritual snobbishness, as if an SJ from the Milltown Institute would be more urbanely dialectical than a CC from the Styx. Like most of his generation, Dad combined religiosity with a slight sardonic anticlericalism. Me, I always found Saint Francis Xavier church a warm and welcoming venue in which to whisper my trespasses.

It was warm and welcoming again the night of Christmas Eve, as I climbed the spiral staircase to the choir in the gallery over the West door. In the headphones of my Walkman set, 'Adeste Fideles', the recessional hymn that has the ring of a boisterous drinking song, was fading for the bulletin at 1 a.m., and the tension that goes with a live transmission was easing in quick lockstep with it. But the first item in the news hadn't to do with papal greetings or stranded airplane passengers. Instead, it reported the tragic death of a person who had, it appeared, driven a car into the water at a harbour within walking distance of the city's brash festivity. Foul play was not suspected. And I suddenly remembered anecdotal word in the late summer of a disabled individual propelling himself in broad daylight off the pier in Dún Laoghaire, for the strongest arms in the world belong to the wheelchair user. 'Happy Christmas', I said to the soprano line, shaking hands but thinking of hands shaking, and the sopranos said it back: 'Happy Christmas to you too.'

It's almost forty years, that strange, estranging biblical passage of time, since two American Jews, Paul and Art, sang a definitive rendition of the Christian carol 'Silent Night' from the corduroy grooves of an old vinyl LP in my bedroom, a lamenting, lullaby-like rendition against a background of radio break-through, a blend of wireless static and sad soundbites from Vietnam and the rioting ghettoes of the 1960s. The glorious 'Adeste' and the sorrowful newscast, up there in the gallery of Gardiner Street church, seemed almost the same for a moment as that Simon and Garfunkel cover from the years of the counter-culture, a contrast amounting to counterpoint: the glad versus the grim, life versus death, just as the hymn sheets for the midnight Eucharist had been printed on the back of a parish funeral form.

But to think so may be to mistake, if not altogether to miss, the paschal nature of the birth of Jesus – 'paschal', that is, from the Greek verb *pascho* with its ancient Attic root-work in strickenness and suffering – just as we can miss the incarnational grandeur of the Passion narratives by confusing another Greek term *agonia*, an athlete's work-out, with our later English 'agony'. We call the solstice holy day the Feast of the Incarnation because for those with a high Christology the history of that happening fills and fulfils the heart. The Word has assumed flesh and, in the Greek idiom of Saint John, has pitched his tent among a travelling people. Then again, for those who fear belief

IN THE POORER QUARTERS

lest it turn out in the end to be make-believe, the birth of a baby, even without the legendary apparatus of angels, still calls for a knees-up if not for a genuflection; while for those who risk the peril of mystification in the exploration of mystery, the story of the stable is a creature comfort. In short, the accent has always been on euphoria. Humanists and Hindus join in the song and dance. It's the season of goodwill because the season itself, the sterile butt of the dead year, is pure spite – which is why, I suppose, we colonised the ancient Roman Saturnalia of late December in the first place, making it, from the fourth century or so, a modern midwinter service-cum-shindig, in much the way that Hanukkah, the Jewish festival of lights, itself a modest encampment in the religious calendar of the house of Jacob, has grown in cultural stature in modern America as a liturgical parallel to Esau's gentile fiesta.

Now I'm no killjoy. I love Christmas, Christ's Mass, the critical density of the day that's in it. I love the hibernatory stupor between Christmas and New Year. I love what the Irish poet Michael Longley once called in a marvellous expression the 'Great Indoors', the breast and bib of one's own fireside, turned away from the threatening world just as South Sea Islanders build their houses with their backs to the ocean. I love the happy maudlin of Christmas memories. Some of my most potent and poignant ones are bound up with small children shifting figures in the crib to make room for Smurfs, Sylvanian families and toy Confederate soldiers. But I know well – or at least I know as well – that the Christmas aesthetic softens steadily into an anaesthetic when its pain is prettified. I know that the crèche in my living room is only a kindergarten, a tutorial in pictures, and that the adult business of incarnation is sitting at an ATM on the street with a Styrofoam cup in his lap, round the corner from where I live, and that the woman on his left-hand side silently withdrawing €100 from her current account is every bit as interesting and gifted and necessitous.

In human terms, in paschal terms, the story of Jesus begins with a terrified teenager birthing onto a futon of straw in a rock cavity amid the incense of the breath of livestock. It begins in Taliban territory, a sectarian state that murders single mothers by stoning them. It begins badly and will end worse – in the public execution of her child as a condemned criminal in a rubbish dump outside the city walls and far away from the world of water sprinklers and microwaves where I move and have my lenient, semi-detached being. It begins with Caesar Augustus, a man who had himself declared a god by acclamation of the Roman senate, and it ends with a queer God who has given us his word that he will enter into the mucous membrane of history in the presence and the person of a speechless human being. From first to last and from start to finish it is a story about the margins and not the mainstream, a story about the wayside and not about the way, a story about the periphery and not about the centre. It is the compass of a flukish, drifting, untrustworthy star and not the co-ordinates of a sensibly stationary one by which rational and enlightened sorts might steer safely. It is, in fact, the yellow star of the scapegoat, the sign of the outsider, the outcast, the outlawed in an Aryan state.

Little wonder then that Marc Chagall, the visionary Jewish painter of the mundane and the matter-of-fact universe should choose to represent the affliction of his folk in studies of the crucifixion, the very 'disaster' – the Latin word for a 'bad star' – that Christians have used to demonise Jews over millenia. Little wonder as well that the Nativity narrative of Luke summons an honour guard of sheer desperadoes – the despised shepherds of inter-testamental Palestine – to visit the puking mite who has been born at the wrong time and in the wrong environment. For this place, this unstable shed, is par excellence a scenario for midwives, yet there are no women present. It is an unescorted birth, labour without amenity. In the same manner and for the same reason, men who are stalwarts in a theatre of atrocity will be absent from the vigil at the cross. The God of the gospels, who is the God of Abraham and the Father of Jesus, affirms life in the real world of horrific reversal, in the upside down of actual calamity. Those who seek to bring Jesus into the world should know beforehand from the example of his mother Maryam that it is work done in darkness, bewilderment and breakdown. And it reaches beyond the recitation of hop-along lyrics on a high holiday to the silence and solitariness of death. We can sift the historicity of these texts all we like, the weave of their traditions and theologies, but we shred their essential witness if we forget that they depict a deity deeply complicit with our nakedness.

Just as the angel Gabriel announces the advent of the Word of God in the person of Jesus to the Virgin Mary, so the same emissary brings the word of God to the prophet Mohammed, syllable by syllable, in the verses of the Koran. Its account of the annunciation concatenates many of the elements in Luke's narrative while resolutely disavowing the divinity – that 'true God from true God' – of the high Christian tradition which Islam would largely oust from its North African enclave. But it strengthens the sense of Mary's unaccompanied travels 'to the East' in a way that reminds me a little of the travail of Hagar, mother of Ishmael, in the Book of Genesis in the Hebrew Bible, and it expresses well the fearfulness of birthing without matronly help in Mary's desire for death as the first contractions come. But her compassionate and merciful God, the shared semitic lord of the three faiths of the family of Abraham, strews ripe dates from a palm tree when she shakes its trunk and a freshwater stream glistens beside her. Like the stone recess of Bethlehem that prefigures the Easter tomb, this later labour of the Virgin occurs, beyond the glance of the great and the good, within the gaze of God. When the handmaid returns after the birth of the prophet Jesus to her own people, they reproach her at the first sight of the infant, and it is the baby in the cradle who in turn rebukes them with articulate speech – 'I was blessed on the day of my birth and I shall be blessed on the day of my death' – in a manner that calls to the Christian mind both the premature fluency of the bar-mitzvah boy at age twelve in the miracle story of the seminar in Solomon's Temple and also summons up the wizened face of the geriatric suckling child, already wise beyond years and eras of mortal time, in so many Renaissance treatments of the theme.

Modernity's image of the infant combines the scrunched features of a foetus at full term with the age of our species – 200,000 years and counting. Our birthrights beckon in the Christ mystery.

Chapter Two
EPIPHANIES

THE FEAST OF THE EPIPHANY, an older event by centuries than the celebration of Christmas, was always an anticlimax in my childhood. The very word 'Epiphany' brought the magical James Joyce rather than the rejoicing Magi to mind, largely because of my father's proselytising enthusiasm for the subversive Dub who had written the longest short story in the English language, calling it *Ulysses*, a title I often misread as *Useless*. *Nollaig na mBan* hadn't made any inroads, either. Since I started life in an Anglophone Redmondite household, I associated that mumbled phrase with reformatories in the Gaeltacht which my mother would sometimes threaten me with, over some infraction of her stricter edicts.

No, January 6 – her birthday, as it happens, replete with gifts of butter dishes from her limitless retinue of children – saw instead the stripping of the tree and the return of the little crib to the dirty attic where it would lie among snorkels, a boxed skeleton, and pink pellets of rat killer until the third week of the next Advent season. So it's wonderful to witness the table-laying of a new, renewing feast day as tens of thousands of Orthodox Christians, Russians, Romanians and Greeks in our metropolitan midst, gallivant for a few whole-hearted hours at the great good news to the Gentiles that the legend of the kings expresses and embodies; for, while the tale may not be factual in a forensic manner, it is profoundly true nonetheless. It's true as story, it's true as his story, the story of a plenary, intervening God, and it's true as *histoire*, the French noun that means not only 'story' and 'history' but also 'love affair', as in the Lord's love affair with the whole of humanity.

It's wonderful as well to welcome the beauty of Eastern liturgy into our multicultural lives, lives that can resemble Babel or Pentecost in direct ratio to our own receptivity towards the advent of the Other. The medieval envoys of the Tsar, who far preferred the Divine service of Constantinople to the Eucharistic rite of Rome and who recommended accordingly that Russia espouse Byzantium instead of the West, chose loveliness over logic. It is true, isn't it, that the Latin rites of the Roman Catholic and the Reform Catholic traditions can strike us at times as pinched, clinical and quickly efficient beside the gradual voluptuousness of the sheer sheet music that Saints Basil and Chrysostom are credited with authoring for the liturgies of the cities of the Pauline epistles. After all, the Way, the Truth and the Life, the semitic trinity that Christians try to imitate in the enigmatic rabbi Jesus, can shrivel and shrink unless we witness also to the Hellenic hat-trick from ancient Athens whose fifth-century philosophy always and everywhere combines the Good, the True and the Beautiful.

There's another threesome to be considered, for the Christian calendar has in its turn always and everywhere associated a trio of scriptural readings in the New Testament – not indeed that there's anything old or obsolete about the testimony of the Hebrew Bible – and those three readings which triangulate so curiously in our tradition comprise the Epiphany (unique to Matthew's folkloric fictionalising), the wedding feast at Cana (a fable unique to John) and the historic baptism of Jesus in the Jordan, a hinge of high importance in all four of the canonical gospels, though in quite conflicting ways. Caspar, Balthazar and Melchior, the mythical royals on walkabout, have monopolised the show for eons, but that archaic tercet of narratives – birth, baptism and banquet – with their parallel and inter-penetrating sense of the waters of labour, the water of a river and the water at a wedding, still rain down blessings in a dry season, even if two of them – the visitation of the wise men and the spontaneous supply of best vintage from a stone cistern – would have utterly puzzled the true-life *hasid* or holy man from Nazareth, whose ministry was spent in the service of the lost sheep of the house of Israel and not the mongrel nations of the Pax Romana. It is most unlikely that Jesus ever waded in the waters of the Mediterranean. The generosity of the mission to the gentiles was the response of his devotees after his death to the radical generosity of the event they named the Resurrection.

Whether the journey ends in Luke's little declivity in the rock face or in Matthew's more upmarket dwelling place, those who follow a long-haired star from the East are by definition an Easter people. The comet of the Christian caravan still trails the same fragile, flickering signal that brought the wise to their knees in the fable of what matters most: promises, pledges, parents, pregnancies, the supreme drama of the damaged human family as the model of our ethical engagement with the unfamiliar world, the navel of reality, God's love assuming flesh in the mutuality of our mating and in the holy communion of our body and blood. The gifts showered on the Christ-child should be bestowed accordingly upon all those planetary persons, male and female, who live and move and have their being in the risk of ordinary relationship: gold for its costly splendour, myrrh as a healing ointment for the hurt that is natural to intimacy, and frankincense as a fragrant sign of the royalty of our affections.

Jesus the Galilean must have loved weddings. He feasted at them and he feasted on them, fashioning their figures of speech into a living image of God's kingdom as a community at profound play in the tenses of the verb 'to be'. Ever since the prophet Hosea, it had been the Hebraic practice to understand Yahweh's love as spousal desire for his people; and doesn't rabbinic Judaism, far from our own Augustinian hesitancy, commend lovemaking on the Sabbath as a local echo of the Lord's outspoken creativity?

Not that Aramaic marriages were any less human than our own. Every bit as arranged as the bourgeois alliances of our professional and post-Christian Northworld are today, in which the theme of real property subsidizes the talk of real presence, weddings in Jesus' time were grounded in communal priorities and not in the primacy of individual passion. Nor should we impoverish the miracle at Cana by reducing it to a gimmick we could easily watch on a variety performance by royal command on a bank holiday broadcast. Even Pharaoh's court charlatans in the book of Exodus were able to turn water into blood without blushing, while theological talk of the institution of the catholic Christian sacrament of marriage is a thousand years too early. The transformation in the story in Saint John's gospel is itself about metaphor and metamorphosis, about a change in deed and not the clever feats of a changeling. Because of the Jews, because of the Jew Jesus, some part of our amino acids has been altered. It is as if the ordinary water of our lives together has been decanted – the stale and the sparkling, the tap water, spring water, rain water, salt water of sea storms, antiseptic of our tears, sweat of our dancing, the stream of time itself in which we are steeped – until the pouring of it fills our mouths with the taste of wine, the sting of rot gut like a paper cut on pursed lips, or like the eucharistic sign of the infant Jesus in Fra Angelico's fresco, busily stuffing his chubby gob with a sprig of grapes.

Isn't this why Christ went down into the waters of the Jordan River, like an Orthodox Jewish woman immersing herself after menstruation in the warm pool of the ritual bath, the mikvah? He was dying to live. He knew that the knowledge of water is not H_2O. It is thirst. It is the swollen tongue in the throat. How long had he been a student in the Baptist's wilderness seminar? How long before he hungered for a diet more sociable than the locust and wild honey of the hermit, and broke with his mentor, imagining bread and wine, a meal rather than food? What were the reciprocities and what were the rivalries between the two actual factions, the entourage of John and the retinue of Jesus, whom the propaganda of Luke presents not only as comrades but as cousins, yet whose utter disparity is the leitmotif of Saint John's great overture? And when and how did the merely messianic intention of the literary device of the dove and the voice at the riverbank become involved in the Trinitarian architecture of the later Christian community?

The immense Lutheran thinker Karl Barth who bestrides the first half of twentieth-century theology scoffed famously at the search for the irreducibly real Jesus, the Torah Talmud rabbi within, behind, beneath the vision of the risen Christ. But the incarnational Christian, at least in the Latin West, cries out to the man himself, to the son of Mary, to the head lice in the halo, to the storyteller under the olive trees, where the long-legged ants among the sheep droppings porter black grains of the lunchtime loaf into their centre-city labyrinths.

We call it a night. Sometimes we call it a nightmare. Joy, when it comes, is harder to bear than unhappiness. We fall flat on our face and disguise it as a religious prostration. That is the way we are made. But we are invited by a desert people to wash in sand, to go down into the water that we came from in the beginning, the original deep that our minds have forgotten but our bodies still remember. For, in the first trimester of our foetal freedom, our rudimentary spines end aquatically in a fishtail. So we descend in order to ascend. We go in thirst that is not as civil as taste and in nakedness that is not as simple as nudity into the risk of renewal through ruin, into the silence of preparation and the speechlessness of reparation, where our lungs must become gills again. We must immerse ourselves in the unfathomable fresh and saltwater of ourselves, where our tears have the odour of sperm and our periods the smell of estuaries, beyond sight of solid ground and dry land, where we can only pray that in this death-dealing, life-giving element, our hearts will sink like anchors in the waters of the firmament and the waters of the uterus, and that we will find our truest, newest natures in each other, in each other's otherness, and in the melting watercolours of Otherness itself.

Chapter Three

RELIGION AND/OR SPIRITUALITY

WHEN I WAS A SMALL SCHOOLBOY in the 1960s, the opposite of the adjective 'religious' was 'irreligious'. During my early college years in the East European bleakness of the new university at Belfield, the opposite of 'religious' altered gradually to 'non-religious'. By the time I became a father in the mid-80s, when the birth of my daughter Laura brought me into the world for the first time, it had changed yet again. Now, if you weren't religious, you were nonetheless spiritual. In fact, if you weren't religious, you were deeply spiritual. Your spirituality was in inverse ratio to your religiosity. You had the cultural prestige of having cut your own path through the wilderness without any assistance from those awful ordinary Christians who fill the smelly churches with their body odours and their bawling children, let alone the bronchial geriatrics on their walking frames who pass wind during the Eucharistic prayer. If you were on your own, you were out on your own. If you stood outside, you were outstanding. You were, as Sylvia Plath says somewhere, the only vertical in a world of horizontals. You were your own man or woman: independent, individual, autonomous, and, most of all, original.

This binary soundbite – spirituality versus organised religion – is still more or less the semantic situation as I speak. And it isn't confined to Christians. When I was a student in the States, I used to hear the same argument from secular Jews who were friends of mine. Utterly erudite in their reading and their critical reflection, these postgrads were quite ignorant of their own traditions and often indifferent to them. They neither studied Torah nor attended the synagogue services. Indeed, there was a time – admittedly in a bar over many Hawaiian Anchor Steam beers – when I recited a psalm to one non-practicing mate of mine who had grown up without his Hebrew Bible, and he asked me where I had got such a beautiful poem from. I told him I got it from him, and he should be ashamed, especially since his name was Cohen, the Hebrew word for 'priest', a person consecrated for proclamation.

The irony was that my drinking pal knew much more than I did about Anglo-Irish literature – Synge, Swift and Sheridan – which is neither here nor there in one sense, but he knew zilch about his own covenant community. He was too busy looking for God out there in the vibratory universe to have realised that God was looking for him down here in the dust and pollen of time, and had already found him and chosen him. He had forgotten, if he ever knew it, that God is not watching from a distance, as that heretical ditty says. God is not the sound of a gong reverberating remotely in inter-galactic space. God is a God of history and a God of human beings, the God of Abraham and Jesus and Mohammed, a God of relationships, a God who is related to us, a God who includes us, all of us, in his/her self-definition, a God who, as the Holocaust survivor Elie Wiesel says, made men and women because he adores stories. And God comes to us, as I read recently in an article, not as megaphone dogma but incognito, 'disguised as weekdays'.

'God comes to us disguised as weekdays.' I wish I'd had written that phrase. I wish I'd written it because it's true and good and beautiful and because my possession of it would, as we say in a revealing expression, 'reflect credit upon me'. I am, you see, a part of my culture and not apart from it, as I used to fancy and to fantasise; and my culture – which is predatory and proprietorial, the lifestyle-with-attitude of the haves in Europe and North America – valorises originality and despises imitation. None of us wants to be a copycat. Each of us wants to be an original. For a writer to be accused of error or bias or obscenity is fine. It may even be a market advantage, if it's manipulated by the right sales team. But to be accused of plagiarism, of the concealed influence of others in the construction of the free-standing self, is social and professional disaster.

Yet we all know in our fibrillating heart of hearts that none of us is original, not even in our sins. Original sin itself is only the poor imitation of other people, the sum of our desires and our resentments copied from their desires and resentments, for even those things – our needs and our wants – come to us from without and not from within. It is an axiom of advertising that the lives we allegedly lead are frequently lives that we follow. Whether in a state of conflict or community, whether popular or polarised, we are plural creatures before we are singular creations, we are social before we are solitary. We are born from others and we will be buried by others; and in between, others, whether as role models or as rivals, as mentors or as tormentors (and usually as both at the same time), will be the gauntlet and the honour guard of our being in the world.

No wonder Jean Paul Sartre, who wanted all his life to be his own work, could write the bittersweet mantra of the call to individuality: *L'enfer, c'est les autres.* Hell is other people. Actually, the reverse is the case. There is no human nature outside human culture. Human nature is the product of human culture. Human nature is evolutionary, experimental and ongoing. It is, as Sartre's sweetheart Simone de Beauvoir remarks in her *Second Sex*, not a biological process but an historical deed. And just as there is no human nature outside human culture, there is no self outside community. And it's only when we see this, not from the tragic perspective of a botched shot at personal empowerment, but from the comic or the comical or, best of all, from the comedic point of view, that we realise our real authority begins in the cheerful recognition that all of us, without exception, are karaoke kids.

There was a time when I knew this. Back in my boyhood, I loved being part of a large family. I enjoyed groups as such: gangs, teams, classes, schools, neighbours, relations – the deep, deciduous human ensembles that comprise a life and its little proliferations. At plays and pantomimes I savoured the slow shaping of an audience into a congregation, as the liturgy of the theatre first formed a crowd into a community and then transformed that community into a communion, just as, swaying at the sub-bass speakers of a Grateful Dead concert in the Greek Theatre at Berkeley and staring up at the stubbled face of the late Gerry Garcia, I would later experience a moment of fascistic ecstasy among the counter-cultural disciples of Dionysus.

Mass was another matter. It was a crowd event without the claustrophobia, community without commotion. Between the entrance hymn and the final blessing, between the *Come see* of the start and the *Go tell* of the close, I sometimes sensed, although I couldn't state it, the sanctification of those around me. I had been taught a literalist doctrine of the Eucharist in which the dedicated bread was radioactive with the risen Christ, and it would be decades before I began to understand that what I had loved obscurely in the packed pews of my infancy was the real presence of God in the Body of Christ all around me: in my grandmother who wore dead animals in a stole around her neck; in my sister wiping lipstick from her mouth as she walked to the altar rails for communion; in the kneeling schoolgirls wedging their mini-skirted behinds against the benches in front of me; in the elderly men who were lost to the world in their black missals and white memorial cards; in the pious housekeeper who had clipped a handkerchief to her hair in place of a mislaid mantilla; in the young man at the back of the nave, skipping the sermon for a smoke in the porch and a look at the paper; and in the green, God-given world of the village beyond the bus stop, where the Lord was carried under a canopy among saluting policemen at the summer solstice each year, past Woods' news agency and Freeney's sweet shop where a penny coin called a denarius bought a wrapped pellet of bubblegum, and past the Ever Ready garage and Keenan's haberdashery where my mum bought brown stockings and a girdle, or was it a garter, with hooks and stinging elastic snaps.

That was a long time ago. The conformist church-going of the 1960s has become the conformist non-church-going of the millennium. I myself abandoned the cult for several years in my early twenties. The telling of stories and the sharing of food, which are the two anthropological aspects of Eucharist, doesn't always consort with the later teenage years when we want to tell our own story and prepare our own meals. It took time, the endurance and duration of years, to discover slowly that the stories in scripture were an autobiographical archive of my own life, of its fertile swervings and its sterile reversals and of its stricken yet surviving vitality. Besides, my faith had remained infantile while I had become first an adolescent and then an adult. I had not allowed or even encouraged it to grow with me into the mortal complexity of a properly mature existence. Apart from the cultural nostalgia, a homesickness of sorts, which saw me altar serving during a sabbatical in San Francisco in the innocent Indian summer of the years before Aids, when the city was a tent of meeting for men who had been demonized elsewhere and had drifted or been driven there because of its faith in the radiant virtue of tolerance, I went my own way. The glamour of solo flight took over. But it was solo flight from what?

James Joyce's *Portrait of the Artist as a Young Man* begins with the magnanimous cadences of the standard mythical recital – 'Once upon a time' – and it ends in the condensed, clandestine notes of a private diary. But the opposite itinerary – from the isolated ego back to the garrulous capital – is, as we know since the publication of *Ulysses* in 1922, a more splendidly pedestrian odyssey. For the Holy Ghost descends not as a Palestinian dove but as a Dublin pigeon.

This isn't to suggest that private prayer is in any sense secondary. Private prayer is as basic to being as are daylight and darkness – or darkness and daylight, to give it the Jewish order. But public worship rests and refreshes our spirituality. It is more than thanksgiving to God. It is giving thanks that we are a community before we are individuals. We are individuals only because we are a community. In today's lectionary readings, the Lord calls Samuel through Eli and he calls the disciples through John the Baptist. We are a sodality grounded in tradition and called by it into profound solidarity with our species, in the radical understanding that the New Jerusalem is the ordinary Nazareth of an inexhaustible seven-day wonder: the mundane and modest domain of the seven days of the week.

Chapter Four

CHRISTIAN UNITY?

THE TRADITIONAL WEEK OF PRAYER for Christian unity occurs in all the major churches at this time. We are still in the middle of it. Whatever ecumenical core group situated its celebration in the last weeks of winter and not in the first flowering of February had a strongly sardonic sense of its timing if not of its timeliness. Great liturgical occasions take place in its immediate aftermath – La le Bríd, Candlemas, and, not least of all, James Joyce's birthday, a dear anniversary which treasures the entrance into this world of a truly Galilean genius and a great incarnational thinker. Of course by 2 February, his date of birth, the prayer week for Christian Unity is long gone, though at least it has the great good luck to climax this year on Wednesday 25 January, the feast of the conversion of Saul the Pharisee/Paul the Apostle, from whom we have the most ancient account of the institution of the Eucharist, the bread-breaking that Christians have squabbled over scandalously ever since the original sitting, if not, as Saint Luke suggests, during it as well. No wonder the Council of Nicaea didn't mention the Lord's Supper in the formulation of the creed we recite on Sundays. If it had, the delegates would still be in plenary session, busily bickering. Perhaps that's why the Salvation Army, in ways a very sensible regiment, smartly averts all the divisiveness inspired by the sacrament of unity by not having Communion at all. The Lord is surely smiling.

Not that ecumenism hasn't made some advances. When I was a child, holding the rabbit ears up high like the priest at the consecration as my family watched *The Riordans*, the Catholic curate in that Sunday series embodied an equally exalted Roman rigour. He was vigorous and virile. On the other hand, his Church of Ireland counterpart epitomised the saccharin caricature of the delightfully dotty rector. The soap that replaced it reversed this cartoon, for in *Glenroe*, as I recall it, the Roman Catholic parish priest played the endearing amadán while his C of I counterpart exhibited the more maturely ministerial strengths. The sociological shift from one type to its mirror-image indicates a rift amounting nowadays to a rupture with our triumphalist ancestral representations of the priest amid his people.

In fact, now that I think of it, I've a notion the Glenroe PP chucked it all in at the end of the day. For what or whom I can't think of, but I suppose it was either Punch or Judy, as my misanthropic granduncle, Canon Joe Mathews, used to mutter to his old-fashioned stock. Uncle Joe, you see, had served as a chaplain at the Somme and he admired the British Army almost as much as his own rather militaristic model of the universal Church with its GHQ in Rome. When the Irish cabinet stood outside Saint Patrick's Cathedral during the funeral service of Dr Douglas Hyde, rather than risk cross-contamination by going in to the alien chancel, my granduncle was off holidaying in England with the Anglican vicar in the same parish, who was also a war veteran.

But this is to reminisce, and reminiscence is usually devious. In the thirty years since Jesuit Michael Hurley first implored fellow Roman Catholics to attend religious services in other Christian traditions once a month for Morning Prayer or Eucharist instead of once in a month of Sundays for a burial rite, the chronic sectarian troika of our history – Papist, Protestant and Presbyterian – has been overtaken by a green godsend of unexpected ecclesial arrivals: Orthodox, Evangelical, African. It's as if the Holy Spirit herself were suddenly sick to death of all our inter-denominational subcommittees with their agreed statements and their laminated conference name-tags, and were saying to us, shouting to us in the mantra of Joyce himself, over the new Nigerian acapella and the Pentecostal testimonials in downtown Dublin, 'Come! Mess!' Meaning 'mess' in the twofold sense of festivity and food: be playful, be ludic, be ludicrous; and at the same time sit together, drink together, eat together. Have done with the dietary laws. Let us all go and consume the bread of the presence that was set aside for the high priest. As Cardinal Newman knew, the only sin of the heretic is the sin of untimeliness.

Now it's easy for me to say this. I'm an ordinary lay Christian and not a cleric, not officer corps. If I were, I'd be court-martialled. Recently, German theologian Fr Gotthold Hasenhuettl (whose name, incidentally, translates as 'rabbit hutch') lost his licence to teach seminarians. He had already been suspended for inviting non-Catholics to receive holy communion at a Mass in Berlin. Truly, as Flannery O'Connor once remarked, those who suffer for the Catholic Church very often suffer from it.

It's not that I'm *a la carte*. I'm strictly *table d'hote*, a bread and wine man. The Lord is my portion and my cup. Even in the depleted form of the sign that my tradition persists in performing, offering bread without wine to the worshipping community, the sacrificial meal is at the centre of my life. It is the cool silence of the airport church in the raucous bustle of my comings and goings, refreshing me and returning me to a world that the Lord saw was very good indeed. But precisely because the quiet hospitality of the sacrament mirrors the hospitality of Christ toward the whole of creation, I know that the Eucharist is made for man and not man for the Eucharist. It is not only the earthly summit of Christian liturgy for which we all strive. It is also the earthy source of Christian living in which we all try to survive. There is eating and drinking in it, or should be. There can also be what you might call Mass hysteria. I speak as a member of a tradition that utterly neglects non-eucharistic services in parish worship.

Adults at real Masses use pretend food. Children at pretend Masses use real food, chocolate buttons if I remember. Teilhard de Chardin reminds us that a person cannot pray unless she has something in her stomach; Bertolt Brecht's version of the same humility was his grand rallying cry: 'First grub, then culture!' Indeed, the Greek word which we translate as 'eat' in the Gospel of Saint John is more accurately conveyed by the vernacular verbs 'chew' or 'munch'.

We cannot be protectionist about the Christian pantry. We cannot mimic the terrible territorial eye-balling of the religious bouncers who police the Church of the Holy Sepulchre in Jerusalem, converting it into a combat zone by their macho aggro over where sanctuaries start and finish. And we cannot give Holy Communion, as Pope Benedict did, to the Protestant Frère Roger, Brother Roger of Taizé, simply because he was a saint. None of us can be qualified or disqualified in that way. It is never a question of membership on merit. If it were, the Eucharist would cease to exist because no-one on earth would deserve it. It is never a question of exclusion, either. Two strong sinners, Peter and Judas, attended the Last Supper as honoured guests though both their betrayals were perfectly predictable to the host. Eucharist is a matter of needy and necessitous people. It is a matter of human hunger and thirst. Ecumenical get-togethers are all very well, but we cannot eat the cutlery, no matter how thoughtfully the table has been dressed.

In church, we stand together under the paternity of God in the human fraternity Jesus models. In our bungled grandeur, we are flawed and awesome creatures who assemble for the same reason that we go to AA meetings: because we are members of a three-legged race who cry out to each other in a brokenness that is more interesting and more beautiful than the silicone spotlessness of the mannequin. We come together because the communion service is the apotheosis of the human outsider. It is a non-violent rendezvous in which we seek the strength – and the weakness – to vindicate all victims without demonizing any victimizers, which is why, I suppose, Bishop Desmond Tutu, leading a Eucharist when apartheid ended, spoke the words of consecration in Afrikaans, for an epoch the demotic of the jackboot and the police permit. Like the two disciples in the theological parable of the path to Emmaus, we recognise the Lord not only in the certified pellets of wheat but in the breaking of bread itself, in the action of community, in an inclusive event without any scapegoats.

Of course there are differences, little and large, in the Eucharistic doctrine of the sibling churches. Their hermeneutical histories vary widely, and these variations do make an iota of difference. But they should not dismay us. There are differences among the four gospels, for goodness' sake. The long journey from Mark to John can take (perhaps should take, if we are truly incarnational), a lifetime of prayer and praxis. But the gracious tension that sustains the four canonical gospels as they dialogue lightly and delightedly in their blessed diversity also informs and transforms individual church traditions. Methodist, Presbyterian, Baptist, Episcopalian, each has its own charisms, its own emphases, its own ages and stages of spirituality, its own particular inflection of the ordinary courtship of the mystery of Christ as humanity's masterpiece and the icon of God.

This is great news, as well as being good news. Polyphony is surely more satisfying than unison. *E pluribus unum*, as the Americans say on one of their coins – out of many comes one. In the double ministry of Peter and Paul, in that gritty and difficult duet between our heritage and our horizon, between apostolicity and catholicity, between human might and divine maybe, the Church must always exceed itself in order to become itself – so the Jewish New Testament is in Greek, the gentiles are welcome, and God is beyond our dogmatic encampments in the no-man's land between our bullet points. Indeed, much to the mortification of the church authorities everywhere, the Father of Jesus is truly beyond the beyond, outside all bounds.

So the aboriginal quarrel between Peter and Paul at Antioch – the who's in, who's out and who's who of the infant Christian community as it drafted its first pass laws – is the radiant precedent for today's full and frank discussion of inter-communion. We are not hostages in our own houses. Home is not like that. Home is home. The content of our tradition forms us. Its form contents us. I love mine utterly. But like every other Christian I am a curate of the future and not a curator of the past. Pilgrimage is the thing. The theology of the quest is our haemoglobin. We are en route among the hostels and the hospices of the several traditional sayings of one and the same Word, a Word that pitches its canvas tent among us nomadically instead of sinking permanent cement foundations inside our breeze-block forts. We are on the way.

In hoc signo vincis or some such slogan triggered the unfortunate conversion of the Emperor Constantine early in the fourth century. If I remember the fable, he saw the Chi Ro emblem, the initial Greek letters of the word Christ, stencilled in the rising sun before a big battle. My granduncle, who remembered dying teenage conscripts calling out to their mothers – Mama, Madre, Mamam, Mutig, Mam – would have liked the tale. But the Chi Ro page in the Book of Kells provides a handier legend for the advance of Christianity in the third millennium. Part of the picture shows a cat and a mouse companionably sharing titbits of bread under the table at the last supper.

Chapter Five
SCAPEGOATS

THE DYING DAYS OF JANUARY mark the anniversary each winter of the liberation of the death camp at Auschwitz by the merciless avant garde of the Soviet Red Army in 1945, when my parents here in Ireland were rejoicing at last in a stable second pregnancy after the unspeakable loss of just one life, that of a first daughter almost at birth. Little Thérèse, whose dubious baptism pointed her towards Limbo although my mother had protested pointlessly to the hospital chaplain that she'd already christened her by desire in the warm lagoon of her uterus, was awarded a liturgy and a burial and even, latterly, an inscription on stone in a cemetery where the grass is cut and the gravel paths are raked. Elsewhere in Europe on the morning of her birth the terraced generations of limitless, eliminated families settled softly as soot, like the photographic negative of snowflakes, on the quivering branches of the Christmas trees that surrounded the chimneys of the crematorium outside Krakow with an evergreen camouflage. There would be another million lives lost before the Holocaust would be doused, in an unbearable irony, by the military machine of a Soviet psychopath who was as mathematical about murder as his Austrian enemy-brother.

My mother and my dad, peace be upon them, had left a list of wedding gifts in Brown Thomas of Grafton Street to be consulted by the guests they were inviting to their marriage feast in the gracious Gresham Hotel in Dublin. As the canteens of cutlery, the bedlinen and the continental lampshades were checked, confirmed and crossed off the typed inventory, higher civil servants with Arts and Science doctorates from ancient German universities congregated at an elegant conference centre at Wannsee to coordinate their forward plans for the terminal deletion of the Semitic element from historic Christendom. It was going to be a logistical nightmare, even for a managerial élite used to succinct solutions, quota pressures and/or incentive-driven productivity. At least they could use the metal track and wooden sleepers of the same locomotive infrastructure that allows my children's friends to inter-rail to Auschwitz with a student's season ticket in this, the dazed third millennium, browsing in the execution ground in their Benetton ponchos and their Sony IPods among what one Modern Languages sophomore reported on a postcard as 'barbed wire, barbed wire, barbed wire'.

No audio exists of that Wannsee think tank and its competitive brainstorming. I suppose the delegates broke up into small groups at some stage before reporting back to the session facilitator, Adolph Eichmann. But you can listen on the Internet to a recording of Eichmann's Chief Executive Officer, sometime schoolteacher Heinrich Himmler, encouraging his subordinates in the good work of industrial genocide at a place called Posen in 1943; and it's strange to listen on headphones at your own PC to the intimate oxide tape recording of his off-the-cuff comments about mass extermination. My parents, Joe and Tottie, had just moved into Nutley Avenue, a cigarette away from where I'm speaking, though their house honeymoon had been somewhat overshadowed by an unfortunate embarrassment. The unmarried maid they'd employed gave birth in her bedroom to a premature child whose arrival had been greatly accelerated by the metal corsetry she wore to conceal her pregnancy. My dad, a good-looking doctor, delivered the baby before in turn delivering them both, mother and child, to a Dublin maternity hospital and, I suppose, to an eventual North of England munitions factory where she probably packed grenades or the ordnance that pilots painted boobs on, giving rise to the endearment 'bombshell' as a certificate of beauty.

I don't mention these things to castigate the parents who moulded me in some shape or form into what I do and what I fail to do. My life does not bear close examination either. I have spent it doing the same sort of perfectly understandable things from the very best of motives, and I shall have to answer for each and every one of them in the fullness of time. That is my privilege and my peril as a responsible human being. In any event, domesticity is only ever a stone's throw from atrocity. Domesticity can itself be atrocity, the sum of stones thrown. Much of my existence has taken place in the introverted sphere of a prudential family life, raising children without a second glance at the processional horrors, little and large, of the corrupt and criminal era in which I've paid my pension instalments, my licence fee, and fretted discreetly about my cholesterol levels. El Salvador, Cambodia, East Timor, Bosnia, Rwanda: all these abattoirs occurred off-stage, on the far periphery of my field of vision, while I was inhaling my daughters' hair and the sweet scent of the nape of their necks in the paddle pool.

The New Testament rightly reprehends those like myself who distort their admittedly important family obligations into an alias or an alibi for their pleasured paralysis in a world of Srebenicas and Sowetos and street fights in Strabane, not to speak of the sadistic, sub-clinical bullying that can go on at the next desk behind the potted plants in the open-plan offices where we work away, noticing nothing. In fact Christianity, our unread, unreasonable religion, has little interest in family values as such, finding the altar wine of community to be altogether thicker than the blood of genetic connection.

Auschwitz, a mnemonic of modernity, begins with A and ends with Z, and the A is no alpha, no grand capitalised Abomination but the little indefinite articles of everyday life. When I was a child, my culture taught me always and everywhere to be wary of Protestant clergymen and of homosexuals. Their marginality made me mainstream. Their eccentricity centred me. Their abnormality proclaimed my normative nature. Today the culture teaches my children to beware in turn of Catholic clergymen and of heterosexual males: just at the moment, oestrogen is good, testosterone bad. Just as gay vicars popped up with a regularity that was almost risible in the permanent police line-up of the Sunday newspapers in the 1960s, so today's condemnatory journalism parades the cartoon monsters of dehumanised priests and perverts. Their faces glitter with our saliva – in part the spit of our self-righteous outrage, in part the drool of our prurient obsessions. For there is a deep and unclean psycho-sexual gratification in the work of revulsion. Disgust is the last costume appearance of gusto. And the print and electronic media pander to and profit from our frothy, foaming incredulity. TV and tabloids are the bully pulpits of a new sacrificial priesthood, as coercive and censorious now as any demonised Maynooth in the olden times, and these incorruptibles preside as prelates over our orgiastic liturgies of condemnation. For the high-handedness of the prince bishops has been replaced in our day by the hauteur of the puritan divines.

Which is to say that everything has changed yet everything is exactly the same as it was. The age-old binary system of our scapegoating society survives all the passing reversals and inversions of mere moral fashion. Its *raison d'etre* is to let us see ourselves as utterly unlike those whom we dislike, to describe and define our authentic human nature over those who do not fully possess it. Just as the only difference between broadsheets and tabloids seems at times to be that the first features small print on large sheets and the second large print on small sheets, so too the perfectly symmetrical conflict between the opposed superpowers in the Cold War, the demonology of my childhood, has been replaced in my middle years by the new reciprocal demonology of Islam versus the West. We think in these terms, and we terminate in these thoughts. It's like subject-verb-object, a grammatical propensity of our intellect, as deep down as the incisors in our mouths and our vigilant hunter's retinas. Nominative-indicative-accusative, which is to say accused, which is to say condemned.

But the black sheep are the lambs of God. This par excellence is the teaching of Judaism and of Christianity condensed into a sentence. The scapegoats are, as the anthropologist René Girard is tired of telling us, the casualties of our rush to judgement and not the culprits of our measured justice. Indeed, the criminal justice system is itself no more than delegated vigilantism, the sacrificial gauntlet of public vengeance. We know perfectly well that prison causes the disintegration of the human person who is the greatest work of art in the universe. We know that all imprisonment in our culture is life imprisonment. There is no redemption from it for one's reputation or for one's rehabilitation. There is only the ridiculed punitive aftermath of lasting disgrace in which the law-abiding rest of us, whose sins are luckily legal, commit time and again the enormous sin against the Holy Spirit – that's to say, the satanic sin of reducing a complex, costly, cherished person, an individual made in the image of God, to the minuscule dimensions of one thing that they have done or not done: one action, one event, one experience. Not alone do we brutalise our scapegoats by representing them as bestial, as animals, as inhuman if not unhuman if not sub-human and therefore altogether non-human, but we insist, as in the case of the current bogey man, the paedophile with his cloven hoof, that he or she or it is incapable of change. This is to insist that he or she or it is not recognisably of our species since change, growth, development, the mystery of the marks of time, are core definitions of what it is to be homo sapiens sapiens in the first place.

If this is all Greek to us, there's good reason. The word 'categorise' comes from an ancient Greek verb meaning 'to bring a criminal charge against'; and the word 'Satan' stems from the Syriac 'Satanas', meaning a legal prosecutor, a court-appointed persecutor. Saint John's expression for the Holy Spirit of the God of Jesus is chosen specifically to counterpoint this, for 'Paraclete' is again an ancient Greek designation for a legal defender, an advocate who stands beside one in the star chambers and the gas chambers of human culture.

The opposite of the criminal justice system, the opposite of public opinion and, God help us, the public demand for something to be done immediately, are the Passion Narratives of the New Testament. They do not describe the juridical, judgemental world from the point of view of the indignant authorities, civil, religious or bureaucratic. They do not expound the social contract or the division of powers or any such stuff, as these things would be understood either by the bench or the bench of bishops, the court of Pilate or the synod of Caiaphas. They do not bang on and on about law and order or the western model of participative democracy. Instead, the Passion narratives demonstrate that, at the end of the high moral road, there is always a gibbet or a hypodermic. They show us what we do as a species when circumstances oblige us to be serious. In short, they reveal the victim, whom we always regard as the victimiser. The three synoptic gospels are so much in sympathy with the object of everyone's loathing that they make it possible for the fourth gospel, Saint John's, to present a condemned criminal who's lost control of his bowels as the subject of the pogrom, and the transcendent subject at that. This is why the birth of the novel coincides with the translation of the scriptures into the vernacular languages of Europe. It's why the novel is strictly a European and a Christian form, because it imagines the Other, not as spook or ogre, but with reverence and deference from the inside-out and not from the outside-in; and so it inaugurates the humanism of individuality.

For almost two thousand years we have been meeting on Sundays to remind each other that the Passion of Christ is our summons to com-passionate the human presence that the mob is massacring. For we know, more or less, that not to do so would be a tragedy – another Greek word, from 'tragou odos', meaning the 'road of the (scape)goat', no different in the dramas of Euripides than in the Book of Leviticus.

The demoniac in the cemetery in Saint Mark's gospel squats among headstones because the community that keeps him captive as the useful plaything of their tantrums and their thirst for blood do not believe that he is really alive in the same way that they are. In fact, they know they are fully human because he certainly is not. When Jesus, who will be demonised in due course and by due process, asks him what his name is, he tells him: My name is Legion, because we are many. He is indeed Legion. He is the fascist, the fanatic, the pouf, the priest, the lesbo, the Provo, the paedophile, the ex-con, the dyke, the kike, the big-nose, the brown-nose, the Opus Dei member, the millionaire, the alco, the nutcase, the nigger, the wog, the wop, the chink in our terrible armour.

Chapter Six
CRISIS

No period of history is more remote than the recent past. There are times when the ruins at Pompeii seem less ancient to me than my own archaic childhood in the Ireland of the 1950s and 60s. When I tell my daughters stories of my schooldays forty years ago in the same Dublin district in which they've also grown up, they're enthralled by stuff that strikes them as ethnic, even exotic. My origins in de Valera's Republic on the point of its first prosperity at the time of the Kennedy visit are as strange to them as the playful seal at Sandycove one summer's evening last year who turned out on closer examination to be a Muslim woman swimming in a long Lycra burka that exposed only her face and her feet.

I grew up in Constantinople and now I am growing old in Istanbul. I am a child of the Council of Trent, a citizen of the late sixteenth century, who came of age during the liturgical reforms of the Second Vatican Council in a time of moon landings and sun holidays, when the parish altar rails that partitioned reality, dividing it like the Berlin Wall between East and West, between Greenwich Mean Time and eternity, between the sacred and the secular, were dismantled and manhandled out into the blinking, workaday world to be sold to designer pubs and public baths. You come across them frequently, just as the frowsy upper storeys of red-brick homes for auction across the capital still secrete their Papal nuptial blessings, holy water fonts, Brigid's crosses, all the faded paraphernalia of a penal and a penalised past. Downstairs there'll be microwaves and remote controls, but up in the scented dimness of the master bedroom, there'll be a portrait of John XXIII and a statue of the Child of Prague beside the packet of Rennies and the bandaged spectacles.

Up to the age of twelve, I slept on the side of my bed to make room for my guardian angel whom I loved and confided in, a tender, taciturn hermaphrodite with its wings folded like ironing boards beside me. Each evening, at the top left-hand corner of my algebra and my spelling exercises, I wrote the words *Ad Maiorem Dei Gloriam*, To the Greater Glory of God, because nothing was so slight or insignificant that it did not reveal God's witty implication in the task of human presence. At home, in the female dispensation of my family, marriage gowns became Holy Communion dresses, mantillas and christening shawls in the great umbilical rope-ladder laundry of generation after generation. Maps in my classroom marked out much missionary green amongst the imperial pink of the British Commonwealth, and if the BBC sought hard information from far-flung, God-forsaken geographies they had only to contact the mother houses in Ireland to be patched through to a Kilkenny accent in Patagonia or a Donegal lilt in deepest Indonesia.

Each morning of the school year, from the days of Sergeant Bilko to those of Sergeant Pepper, I would cycle two miles uphill to the priests' house where my Jesuit masters lived, and there, in a tiny oratory that overlooked a tennis court awash with cherry blossom, sycamore seeds, or the terracotta rugs of the ember months, I'd assist the celebrant in squeezing Jesus into a cup of cooking wine and an edible plastic poker chip over the most grandiose Latin incantations as the kind smell of bacon and egg rose up, like the odour of sanctity, from the refectory directly beneath.

Transubstantiation itself was merely the technical and theological term for a loveliness that was happening to the whole of the hospitable cosmos as the good body of Creation, animal, vegetable and mineral, first turned towards and then turned into the holy mystery of the God who is love. And when I became a lover and then a father in the fullness of time, the priests explained to me on our lunchtime strolls around the school grounds, I too would be able, at the end of the dreadful twentieth century, to take and bless and break and give the bread that my own children had baked that same day in our oven to the little community at my family table. Once upon a time, they would insist, the wings of their soutanes ribboning behind them in the stiff salt breezes, we will live happily ever after. It would only take a revolution here and a strong-arm synod there to usher in unqualified Utopia.

Even at fourteen years of age, I think I may have known this was not going to happen. I had grown up on one of the more self-important roads in south Dublin, among many embassies, where insecure rich folk founded their fragile attempt at self-esteem on the sands of the envy shown to them by others. They left their curtains open at night so that passers-by could see in. But the dialectic of power, prestige and profit did not prevent my leafy avenue, with its gravel drives and its tradesmen's entrances, from its own share of murder, manslaughter, suicide, alcoholism and wife-beating. I was loved into the world, not by my biological mother but by a young woman living in our home who had herself been raised as an orphan in a religious institution, just as I am married now to the lovechild of a West of Ireland teenager who boarded the boat for Britain in the 1950s. Like everybody else, I knew something of the Hidden Ireland long before the funeral games of Irish Catholicism at the Papal Mass in the Phoenix Park and even longer before the disgrace and effective disestablishment of the Church at the end of the millennium.

Despite the self-absorption of puberty, I understood obscurely as a boy that neither the Republic of Ireland then nor the Republic of Letters now nor the Roman Catholic Church at any time in its two-thousand-year-old infancy can claim a close resemblance to the Kingdom of Heaven – or, as theologian Mary Grey charmingly calls it, the 'kin-dom' of heaven, the close community of love. There were houses in my pre-conciliar parish that were smaller than my unshared bedroom at home. I would see queues of children standing in their pyjamas in the street as their tireless parents re-assembled the bunk bedding inside the cottages. As the first beloved hairs began to grow their masculine stubble on my chinny chin chin – helped into visibility, be it said, by the adroit application of my older air-hostess sister's mascara – I heard that paramilitaries in the North of Ireland had used an acetylene torch on the genitals of an informer. But the Southern polity to left and right of me was itself a stratified statelet, a brutalized combat zone of class division. 'Who owns the police?' I asked my father when I was small and a guard had come to the door because of noises at the far bottom of the garden. 'We do', he told me, and I knew immediately what he intended by the use of the first person plural. He did not mean We. He meant Us. The noises at the bottom of the garden, on the other hand, came from Them, like the proletarian boy who gate-crashed our tennis club disco and danced by himself in a fury of self-affirmation as the parquet floor emptied around him in consternation.

One day, in my late and learned godfather's house, skimming through a lavishly illustrated catalogue of the works of the painter Botticelli in search of some gratuitous goose flesh, I came across his annotated judge's copy of the Maintenance of Prisons Act, 1947, in which appeared a detailed description of the medically supervised legal floggings of inmates in Mountjoy Jail, and I understood for the first time why it is that we conceal the loot in our safes behind large oil paintings. Culture is the beauty board that screens the rising damp and the dry rot of our violence and our victimisation. Violence and victimisation are our meat and potatoes as a species. If it were not so, the worldwide entertainment culture of our civilisation wouldn't feature retribution, revenge and retaliation as its primary plotline. For film and TV are only the latest liturgical forms of the sacrificial bloodshed that constitutes civil society, while the only decent blood in the human economy – menstrual blood – is prohibited as utterly objectionable on pain of an adult rating.

All insight is hindsight. I never realised at the time that the devotional culture of my childhood – the sins, the saints, the incense, the world of the BVM in the time before the BMW – was in large part the artificial creation of the nineteenth-century Irish Church, the so-called Cullenisation of the faith by Cardinal Paul Cullen, Romanist and disciplinarian. I didn't know as a kid that Irish writers had been evangelically critiquing the pride and presumption of the national Church for at least a century before my birth, or that the old scores which would be settled so savagely in my middle years between pastor and people across the country had their bitter roots in the eighteenth century, in the British government's creation of Maynooth to forestall French influence, in the gradual supremacy of an enthroned clergy thereafter, and in the eventual disappearance, during three triumphalist generations, of the aboriginal linkage between a persecuted people and their persecuted priesthood. Those in religious life and the secular clergy had taught and tended us, minded and mended us, for two hundred years. It was inevitable that their authority would degenerate eventually into mere power, inevitable too that our gratefulness would mature into grievance, so that now, as we consume and cannibalise ourselves like a shark wolfing its own flesh wounds in a storm of blood, we emerge into a post-religious landscape in which my generation has largely apostatised, in which small children can be terrified of churches because they associate them only with funerals, and in which bewildered adults can be forgiven for fearing that there are more priests in prison than in seminaries – and this at the very moment that the anthropologists are telling us that religion creates society and not vice versa.

All of this is news, none of it is new. There will always be more Amens than Alleluias in human discourse, more Kyries than Glorias. We are radiant but we are radioactive too. The bad old days, as Brecht reminds us, should be set aside so that we can start to concentrate on the bad new ones. The liberal ideal of the perfectibility of human nature through human culture is no longer an illusion. It is a delusion. In a hundred and fifty years we have lost our native tongue and our native faith. Silence, exile and cunning, the stratagems of Stephen Dedalus in Joyce's *Portrait*, must replace language, nationality and church. We are called, like the Swiss Family Robinson, to transform our shipwreck into a tree house, to invent a new ecology for an altered climate. The Christian of the future will be Karl Rahner's model of the individual mystic on walkabout, a man who reads newsprint and scripture side-by-side, a woman who lives and moves and has her being in an asymmetric and conflicted relation to the terrible gods of the state. But doubt is altogether more humanising than certainty. Convictions can imprison us, and they have. Half of the New Testament is a tirade against organised religion. In the Hebrew Bible, the first five books of Moses institute religious cults and codes, and the prophetic books that follow castigate them for their hollowness and obesity. For the real Judeo-Christian remains a tragic optimist who is full of nostalgia for the future.

My Jesuit prefect of studies in secondary school was ordained by John Charles McQuaid with all the sclerotic sacerdotal ceremonial of the age of Pius XII, the last in a line of stiffening pontiffs whose Hundred Years' weariness has been termed the 'Pian monolith'. There was chrism and chanting, prayer and prostration, Latin and unleavened bread, the plenary, preconciliar mode of majesty. Hours afterwards, this sudden, stunned Melchizedek cycled out from Ranelagh to Sandycove for a summer swim in the men's pool where an English regiment, the Fortieth foot, had bivouacked for military manoeuvres a hundred years before. As he undressed, friends and fellow-swimmers came up out of the shining water, naked and new, to kneel before him for a blessing, and he, naked and new in turn, under the blue apse of the sky and the choirs of seagulls, blessed and benedicted them.

At the present time, the believing community is meeting in the same manner, leaders and followers, ordained and lay, all of us reprobate, none of us elect, in an intimate and naked way on the very shoreline where the good waves smash open their molecules of oxygen against the hard margins, where life can begin again in mould and moss, in tiny invertebrates, in the stench of salt and bladderwrack, and in the forty shades of the green seaweed with its healing iodine and its liminal, medicinal phosphates. These are the baptismal sluices that should rule our lives as we re-invent ourselves.

Chapter Seven
HALF A HUNDRED

To have turned fifty, as I did last January, the month of the doorkeeper, is a more impressive feat in the Irish language than it is in English: the fricative tint of the Anglo-Saxon adjective *fifty* makes it somehow sound silly and slight, whereas the idiomatic *leath céad*, half a hundred, has a solid dental cadence, an adult tone about it.

There are times, then, when the calendar seems almost to embody a kind of curriculum vitae, a record of travelling and ravelling. I have hit fifty, and fifty has hit me. When my father, a traditional paterfamilias who had been bred by Victorians, stood at the family fireside on the day of his half-century in 1964 and stared off into the immeasurable responsibilities of the middle distance, I recall thinking as an eight-year-old child that someday I too would possess that gravity and that grace, because God was my father and my father was God. I never imagined that I would watch him, in his ga-ga, geriatric months, dribbling into the remote control of the television set as he sought to phone his favourite truant son in Australia, or that the advent of my own fiftieth birthday would find me as bewildered and dependent as the bespectacled preparatory pupil in school cap and short pants. Perhaps that's why the Holiness Code of the Land of Israel in the Book of Leviticus proclaims a jubilee time of rest and refreshment after seven times' seven years of diligent tillage and pasture, of toil that was understood by the House of Jacob, in the earliest ecological testimony that I know of, to be a form of plunder and pillage that must periodically be atoned for.

The last time I had as strong a sense of thankfulness and gratitude was on my wedding day, a quarter of a century ago, when I found myself to be lost, to be speechless in a twofold manner at the high table, and to be wholly overcome by my new and signal station as a link, a ligature, a length of mucous membrane in which the past, the present and the future met momentarily yet momentously. I was a giddy man-child in a rented morning suit amid the cherry orchard of my friends and family but the whole and holy entourage of the dead and the unborn generations surrounded me in their precious chasubles of flesh, in the infrared of the multitudinous bodies I had descended from and in the ultraviolet of the multitudinous spirits that the future would continue to embody in the vitality of time, in the tenderness of the temporal order, in the endurance and duration of our graced nature. It is not the case, as the Russian proverb has it, that no-man prays for his great grandparents. I prayed to and for all eight of mine by name on the morning of my wedding, understanding suddenly that the dead are even more real than the living because we are in Christ but they are with God.

And so it was no great source of surprise to me when, on the long night of the summer solstice last year, while awaiting the results of hospital tests, I dreamed that, as I crossed the bridge at Donnybrook, I turned left into the late nineteenth century and knocked for admittance on my great grandfather's front door on Anglesey Road. The long-haired ten-year-old child who opened it was my grandmother. She brought me in, took my clothes from me, and seated me at the fire. Outside, in the flooded garden where I would play beside the Dodder river decades later, the laden branches of the apple trees beat against the windows so noisily that we could not hear each other. Instead I signed to her in the language of the deaf and dumb that she would give birth in the fullness of time to my father Joe and that already she was the living image of my second daughter, Lucy, the windfall of my later thirties. Still the branches beat like bodhráns on the thin glass of the sash window. I was afraid it would crack and cloud at any moment like a tablet in water. Pertly and prettily my granny went on laughing, hiding her face from me in the apron of her pinafore. When I woke to the bustle of nurses and the clatter of breakfast trolleys, I could smell her skin again, where my face used to sink into the fat of her cheek, for the first time in forty years.

Leaving the daydream of the ego and the dreamtime of the id for the plain and lucid light of the quotidian domain, what would I say now to my own two children, my own two daughters, who began as my branches and mature as my roots, that I couldn't say in my subconscious to the little Loreto schoolgirl of the 1880s who had, after all, squeezed her own way down the pulsing tunnel of a birth canal with a full store of microscopic eggs in the cushioned tissue of her nine-month-old ovaries, and whose exact copy, a resemblance amounting to doubleness, would assume flesh in another century, in another millennium, as an autumn infant? I would say something like this.

Laura and Lucy, may you pitch your tent always and everywhere in the Eastern Mediterranean and in the gospel of its geography. May you live always and everywhere not in any of the New Jerusalems or in their blinding, antibiotic chancelleries but in *Galil ha goyim*, in the good Galilee of the Gentiles, in the mixed and multicultural immediacy of the hybrid, the mulatto and the mongrel, where Our Lord, whom Muslims call *Ruh Allah*, the Spirit of God, went on walkabout in the ordinary world. May the three semitic faiths, Judaism, Christianity and Islam, stand before you in their individual delicacy and in their sibling strengths as the three angels of Mamre in the Book of Genesis stood before the patriarch Abraham for a breaking of bread and a foot-washing. In the chapter called 'The Table', the Koran itself tells us that 'God could have made us one nation, but it is his wish to prove us by that which he has bestowed upon us. Vie with each other in good works, for to God we shall all return and he will declare to us what we have disagreed about.'

Amid all the polemic of the critics and the preaching of the homilists and the paradigm shifts of the exegetes, keep faith with the paschal rhythm of life and death and rising again, which is the metronome of our patience and our passing and our passion. Read Mark. Listen to John. Remember that most of your reasoning will be rationalisation. Like the post-exilic Hebrews in the sixth century and the post-religious Greeks in the fifth, cleanse your pantheon annually. Be sun-struck. Seek the strangest of gods in the simplicity of crisis. Be not afraid: dawn is a very grey area. Each breakdown is also a breakthrough. Back in 1970 when I was fourteen, a thousand Jesuits worldwide left the Order in a single year, and I remember the desolation certain of my teachers experienced at the sight of this exodus because they had forgotten what Exodus means. They had forgotten the strong arm of the Lord and the hilarity of the spirit, as hundreds of committed men moved into an even more demanding daily ministry in the dormitory suburbs. So, live and move and have your being among the glittering meltdown of images, their waterfalls and their well water, for they are blessings that the heavens have rained down upon us. Be the iconophile of Jesus and the iconoclast of God. Let the unimaginable Father be recognised in the filial face of the selfless son. Let our divine paternity be revealed to us, horizontally and not vertically, in glimpses and not in gazes, in our fraternal smile, in a fellowship that dreams its way, beyond the dull average of mere association, towards the sodality of gladness.

In the Pentateuch beloved of Rabbinic Judaism and in the prophets beloved of Gentile Christianity, find the whole-hearted heritage of the singular Jew whose ministry embodied both traditions, ethics and martyrdom, the systolic and the diastolic motions of the one beating heart. At a time when Shi'ite Islam has been performing its own victimary passion play on the feast of Ashura in the month of Muharram, memorialise the Passion especially. It is the chrysalis. It is the deep rendezvous. Despair too plays its part in the divining and in the divinizing of our nature. In your own lives you will wear many masks in the dramas of naming and shaming. Do not necessarily aspire to the humility and the humiliation of the lead role, for victimhood itself can be the alias of victimisation. Yet, in prayer and praxis, always be rehearsing the two or three dilemmas where you will be invited to choose between fist and fang on the one side and pacific imbecility on the other, as the tuning fork of eternity itself. But be appalled by the cross. When I summoned it up on my workplace PC the other day, Grunewald's Isenheim Christ, a hedgehog full of briars and brambles, was firewalled straightaway, and the legend on the computer screen read: 'You are attempting to view a pornographic image.' May it always be so. May the aesthetic representation of violence never anaesthetise our horror at the serial human holocausts which are the basis of an exclusionary social order. For nothing is true, as Albert Camus reminds us, that forces us to exclude.

Laura and Lucy, you are seeking to construct your existence as a canal, the shortest distance between two points. But God is dreaming of your life as a river, with twists and cataracts and fords and shallows. We cannot pray that it won't rain on sports day, but we can pray that our humanity is deepened rather than diminished by the things that we do and the things that are done to us. We cannot pray to live in the moment, which is dementia and not attentiveness, but we can pray to live in the Eucharistic hospitality of the whole table of tenses, visible and invisible light. We can live, in short, between the future understood as the sacrament of encouragement and the past understood as the sacrament of forgiveness, in the charity of present possibility. So

I wish you both, my two beloved children who have reconciled me to myself and to my parents, to my life and to the eventual leaving of it, what the Lord spoke of in his own oblong, oxymoronic, paradoxical way, when he conjoined the innocence of the dove and the wisdom of the serpent. I wish you the same trust and irony; for trust without irony will break God's heart and irony without trust will break ours. Like youngman Eutychus in the Acts of the Apostles balancing precariously on the window ledge between Paul's prayerful pep talk to a roomful of listeners and the vernacular glamour of the market street outside, may you too find your feet on the shoreline between the good demotic and the skills of stillness.

From the moment of your real baptism, which will be closer to thirst than to fonts and freshets, you will be propelled 'immediately', as Saint Mark likes to insist with his frequent use of the word 'euthus', into a desert experience, into the wilderness of the deep and evolutionary interior. God will enter your life there as a disaster. Your loneliness will grow around you like a monastery. This is not all, but it is everything. For, as my teacher, the poet Denise Levertov used to say to me, if you bring the Lamb of God into your living room, he will almost certainly ruin your carpet. There will be incommunicable spaces of pain and insight within you which have been set aside by God as the pavilion of his presence, like an oxygen tent or like the tent of meeting itself, for the most intimate of encounters.

Chapter Eight
THROUGH THE ROOF

TODAY'S LECTIONARY READING from the book of Mark (2:1-12), the earliest of the four canonical gospels, whose contents were collected and edited within forty years of the death of Jesus, tells the dramatic and quite theatrical story of the poor paralytic. His four friends can't work their way through the crowd, so they devise a wonderful dodge, digging through the turf roof of the house, and lowering their pal like a Greek god in a play by Sophocles into the centre of attention where the Son of Man, the Son of God, God the Son, is sitting on his behind on the mortal earth of a one-room house in a two-horse town called Capernaum. Alternatively, you might argue that a group of guys are unable to access Jesus because he's surrounded and stonewalled by all the religious authorities, the scribes, the Pharisees and the *nomodidaskaloi*, the expert interpreters of the Law of Moses, whose hierarchical rivalries can sometimes work inadvertently to impede worship and witness, rather than to expedite them.

Either way, it's a scene that works wonderfully well on stage, in large part because it's shaped by the conventions of classical dramaturgy as well as by Mark's theological motives. In each of the three synoptic accounts of the same event in Peter's house that Jesus had commandeered as a Galilean headquarters, the finale concludes, as every Athenian dramatic climax should, with a choric celebration of the events that have been represented. Mark's chorus are amazed and glorify God; Matthew's, ditto; while Luke the gentile and therefore the evangelist most at ease with Hellenistic values, the outsider who will put a quotation from Euripides' Bacchae into the mouth of the Hebrew God in the Acts of the Apostles, stresses the crowds' religious awe – *eplesthesan phobou*; they were filled with fear – because *phobos*, our phobia, is one half of the Aristotelian outcome of the sacred liturgy we nowadays describe as theatre. The other part is pity.

Capernaum with its synagogue isn't a hundred miles from the playhouse in Sepphoris, one of the Greek towns in multicultural Galilee in the days of Rabbi Jesus, the itinerant prophet of the end-time during the Roman occupation. But the few footloose kilometres that bring you from one place to the other, from the world of Judaic religious apartheid to the hybrid dust cloud of paganism and polytheism, would have required that the carpenter be a cosmonaut as well as a star-child. I used to love to imagine that a man as frank and free-spirited as Jesus would have roamed beyond the grid of cultural routine to the point where he might even have attended a production of a great Greek classic in the stalls at Sepphoris. After all, the fifth century dramatists were working within intellectual earshot of the post-exilic priestly committees who standardised the Jewish scriptures at the same time, and both these major meditations were embarked upon similar, in ways identical, business. The whole of the Eastern Mediterranean was moving simultaneously toward a marvellous monotheistic vision which would eventually privilege ethics over metaphysics and thereby inaugurate Judeo-Christianity, the breast and bib of who we are. Why wouldn't Jesus have watched Euripides' *Trojan Women*, his Kyrie for the civilian victims of history which is so semitic in its advocacy of the humanity of the enemy whom we caricature, and was accordingly booed, banned and then banished altogether by its first male, middle-class audience in the theatre of Dionysus? Why couldn't Jesus have come fresh from a reading of Second Isaiah, the core of his contemplative life, to a masked performance of Sophocles' *Antigone* whom the Jewish mystic Simone Weil once described as the fifth gospel?

The hard beauty of the historical critical tradition of the last hundred years has taught us irreversibly that Jesus, as a Talmudic scholar who danced with the Torah scrolls in a mood of tenderest reverence, could never have envisaged an outright mission to Gentile aliens. It was Israel he cherished, and those within the house of Jacob who had been jettisoned as riff-raff or recidivists by the Curia in Jerusalem. Foreigners were a skirted, secondary cohort. The rebarbative boorishness of Jesus' riposte to the Syro-Phoenician petitioner may or may not be historical, but it is indicative. Monsignor Meier, the outstanding American exegete, regards it as a creation of the later Jewish-Christian Church, while Oxford's Jewish scholar Geza Vermes, if I recall correctly, inclines to credit the meeting as a possible actual occurrence which has been developed and redacted over time.

In the same way, the Capernaum narrative of the paralytic who is first lowered and then raised, first abased and then exalted, is no pristine anecdote preserved in first-hand reportage by an eyewitness, but a complex doubling of two dove-tailed digests: the one a miracle tale, the report of a major healing by the holy man, the other a missionary epitome of a keynote theological conflict over forgiveness, over the licence to practice leniency, over the healing of sin that parallels the curing of illness. 'Who but God alone can forgive sin?' is the cry of the crowd, the cry of the criminal justice system, the cry of the victimiser and the violent and the violator. But the text is telling us that we can, and must do. The text is telling us that the cultural quarantine in which the paralytic finds himself is a libel against God who cries out for inclusion.

Just as I find the story of the Syro-Phoenician woman persuasive precisely of Jesus' rude rebuttal, so too the unlikely and paradoxical details of the chronicle of the paralytic suggest an earthen base in time and space to its unearthly beauty and intent. At the instant of supreme crisis in a Greek play, when the human predicament is most irresolute and threatened, the

Olympians are always flown in, and they're flown in from what we continue to call 'the gods', the dark overhead labyrinth of winch and wire above the proscenium arch. Whether as Hermes or Athena, Aphrodite or Herakles, their literal arrival out of the blue, their spectacular descent from on high in their 'per-sonas', the elongated wooden masks they wore above technicolour vestments, signalled the impresarial high point of a hit show, a matinee masterpiece. Mere mortals down below, watching at ground level in amazement and paralysed by the sight of such heavenly splendour, would await the immediate cure of all their woes and the renewal of universal welfare before the final frenetic sing-song at the end of the drama, just as two twelve-year-old friends of mine playing dilatory tennis on a public court in Rathgar in the early summer of 1963 looked up at the sudden sound of helicopter rotors swiftly descending over them, their flattened hair, their flapping skirts, to see for seconds a transcendent presence, a *deus ex machina*, a god in a machine, leaning out and smiling down upon them with all the mischief of Massachusetts, as John Fitzgerald Kennedy lit up the rest of their lives with an emperor's wave of the hand.

We speak on occasion of doxology, which is the formal praise of the Lord in public worship, the recitation of his titles and attributes. But the story of the paralytic reminds us that the Judeo-Christian understanding of God's nature goes beyond doxology into paradoxology, if I may invent the word for one opportunistic moment. Paradox is indeed everywhere in this parable. Luke himself uses the word when he has the religious connoisseurs exclaim at the close of the action, 'We have seen "paradoxa", strange things, today'. In fact, their religious doxology – which is deeply respectful and sincere – cannot metabolise such paradox as the proper behaviour of God, cannot gravitate in this topsy-turvy, upside-down world where ordinary human affliction has taken the place formerly occupied by deity, and where divinity, utterly benign, utterly non-belligerent, has become hominised and humanised in the person of a chap lying on the ground in a hut, at ease on the beaten humus of the workaday world. An old Hasidic story that Jesus would have enjoyed tells us that, if we can't discover God in our lives, we're probably not looking low enough. The four friends of the paralytic – whose faith is in reality faithfulness to their incapacitated mate, and therefore loyalty rather than belief – don't have to storm heaven, the high places of mythological Paradises and divine encounters, the rain clouds and cosmic distances of rococo Valhallas. Down here, right here, is the dizzying height. All we have to do is to come down to earth, to excavate the ceiling – literally to dig through it – and to re-enter the world. Luke, always the encourager, improves on Mark's proletarian presentation of the house, replacing sods of turf in the roof-work with gentrified ceramic tiles, as expensive then as they are now, and upgrading Mark's dirty straw mat on which the sick man lies to a more bourgeois bed. Matthew, being strong on dignity, omits the escapade as inappropriate.

But the whole thing is about interiority, of course, and not about interior design. As Karl Barth famously stated, it is about the revelation of God as the abolition of religion. The poet Rilke is even pithier, as poets tend to be: 'Hiersein ist herrlich', he says. 'To be here is manly.' It is also immediate instead of mediated. Mark uses the Greek word for immediately, straightaway, at once, without delay or deflection, three times in this shortest of short stories. For the immediate, the here and now, is so timely it is eternal. It is the atrium of the kingdom of heaven, 'the kin-dom of heaven', the community of love, in which Jesus can address the paralytic as a 'teknon', a child, and in which Mark can speak of 'sins', little particular infelicities, rather than sin with a capital S as a sombre ontological state befouling us all.

So the story of the paralytic is a kindly incarnational text, a word to the wise about the assumption of flesh as the precondition of all purity, just as the historical critical method attempts a more incarnational project than some of its sardonic practitioners may suppose. Of course, the narrative also records a failure to heal. The ironic dialectic of healing and not healing at the same time recurs as a binary scriptural structure. An educated élite, portrayed by Mark as being in dialogue with their own thoughts and reservations, *dialogizomenoi* – in ruminant mode, as it were, with the several stomachs of scholarship – are in reality, like every religious magisterium, the monologists of their own preconceptions. They are in search of perfection and so must miss out on completeness, much as perfectionists always will.

I watched my mother die of Parkinson's disease. In Latin they call it *paralysis agitans*, an agitated paralysis, an immobilised shuddering, a quivering inertia. In my own two years or so in a psychiatric hospital, *paralysis agitans* seemed a good if grim description of the catastrophic self-loathing that lies at the heart of all depressive illness. Whether it's neurological or biochemical, then, the affliction of paralysis, of prostration, exemplifies a foundational fragility in our species. We seize up easily. We are stricken and panic stricken. Just as the four gospels in their different ways lower our human woundedness into plainspoken sight before the gaze of God and away from the easy rhetoric of religiosity, so the whole Judeo-Christian tradition bows down before the mystery of suffering here on *terra firma* where we are graced and grounded. Thinkers as different as Nietszche and Weber link all of this to the politics of self-pity in a small and struggling culture that empires endlessly invaded. But the story of the paralytic, in the ironic reversal of all protocol, in the precedence of love, in the act of God's grasping us before we even ask it, seeks instead to hallow human affliction as the only sanctuary in which the Lord has any interest. So the room in Peter's house brings us, in fourth wall fashion, to the scene of our own apotheosis.

Chapter Nine
AS THE DAYS LENGTHEN

WHEN I WAS A TEENAGER in the late 60s, it took a brave person to go without their ashes on Ash Wednesday. Now it's the opposite. A Hindu wearing a pottu on the forehead will be greeted with all the obsequious solemnity of the post-religious, left-liberal house of fashion, while a sooty stain between the eyebrows at the start of the season of Lent would be the murderous mark of Cain if it weren't already a mark of, well, black comedy, a proof of pig-ignorant provincialism, arousing benign derision among one's office colleagues. Curiously enough, the people in Human Resources will speedily sanction any sneering at turbans or prayer mats, because one part of the Western way is to despise its own traditions as an exercise in freedom while adulating others as the acid test of its own educated sensitivity – and therefore of its claim to cultural superiority. The fact that three days of the week in the Irish calendar refer explicitly to self-denial for the purposes of personal enlightenment – *Dé Céadaoin*, the first fast, *Dé hAoine,* the great fast, and *Deardaoin*, the day between the two fasts – is at this stage only an antiquarian linguistic allusion. In the absence of a counter-cultural, celebratory Lenten disposition in the institutions of Church, lone individuals now have to go the long way round in the search for the skills of stillness; and, in the absence of prompts and pointers, it can take them half-a-lifetime to discover that the consolations of asceticism are more pleasurable and more productive than those of excess.

But I don't want to bang on about mortification or make a meal of it. I have at home a poster-size copy of the Lenten regulations for the archdiocese of Dublin in 1956, the year of my birth, and its small-print columns of power, paranoia and prohibition make very sad reading half a century later. But instead of demonising the defenceless dead, I want to consider an ancient sodality of prayerful persons for whom fasting – in their case on Mondays and Thursdays – was one mode among many others of the dedication of their brotherhood to a personal God who had intervened in history with loving kindness to rescue and redeem them time out of mind over long ages of persecution and scarcity; and I'm speaking, of course, of the Pharisees, the hemming-and-hawing chorus of my prejudicial childhood, who were always represented to me as a central-casting coven of venomous opponents, all hate and hook nose, whom the good Lord would surely have vaporised if he'd used his inter-galactic arsenal of heavenly powers instead of being so infuriatingly meek and mild the whole time. So, two thousand years later, when a gentile friend, a 'shabbes goy', lit lights or turned on oven switches for a Jewish neighbour on the Sabbath, it seemed terribly silly to a little Catholic boy like myself who spent his bicycle rides to and from school uttering scores of pious ejaculations so that my grandmother's sentence in Purgatory would be remitted by a week, a fortnight, a month, or, in the case of 'Sweet Heart of Jesus, be Thou my Love!' by 300 consecutive days.

Yes, my godfather had brought me at twelve or thirteen years of age to a performance at the Gate of Conor Cruise O'Brien's one-person piece *King Herod Explains*, with the late Hilton Edwards playing the corrupt and portly tetrarch in an exculpatory mood; but, no, the author's suggestion, either in the playscript itself or in the programme note, that the historical Pharisees of the first century resembled earnest cloth-cap London School of Economics undergraduates who read the *New Statesman* as if that weekly Labour magazine were sacred scripture, must have been mistaken. Weren't they really homicidal legalists plotting the assassination of the Second Person? No wonder my father had told me that the Jews in Dublin founded their own golf club because none of the Christian eighteen-hole courses would have them. No wonder either that the Lord, living as he did within shank's mare of a theatre, called his religious adversaries 'play actors' which is all that the Greek noun 'hypocrite' means in Matthew's gospel. He could have called them a lot worse; or could he?

We know nowadays that the Pharisees were in fact a pastoral intelligentsia who missioned, much like the best of the Red Guard cultural revolutionaries in Maoist China, among ordinary, wall-fallen folk as they sought to embody, in depth and detail, the biblical *mitzvot*, the diverse daily mandate of observant Jews. Like their confrere, the tentmaker Saul of Tarsus, they earned their livelihood by a useful trade while seeking to demonstrate that it was possible to live religiously in any secular calling. Josephus, their near contemporary, tells us that they had the multitudes on side and that those living in towns would testify to their virtue in devoting themselves to excellence in their preaching and their practice. Indeed, he even remarks that they were guided by the Logos, a term which my own tradition of faith would embellish and beautify as a key Christological term, but which connoted for them the clarity of reason, of light and lucidity as a plenary principle in both Creator and creation.

This isn't to deny that Jesus of Nazareth made many enemies, or that he so antagonised and alienated the religious authorities that the secular power became fatally embroiled in the controversy; but it is to remind ourselves that the representation of the Pharisees in the Gospels may well reflect aspects of transmitted eyewitness accounts of debate and discussion during the public ministry, but they also reveal a very human state of reciprocal hostility, of heartfelt, retaliatory loathing, in the later decades of the first century between the Jewish Christians we derive from and the orthodox rabbinic moderates who had ejected the Jesus entourage forcibly from their traditional places of worship, Temple and synagogue, as a coterie of heretics who ought not to be reckoned among the righteous but instead be blotted out of the book of life. To be shunned by the community, to move from the umbilical world into a blinding limbo, is a short route to bewilderment; but there's an apt irony in the recognition that the New Testament scriptures which examine themes of exclusion so massively and so meticulously should themselves be marked in many places by the structuring resentments of men who believe themselves to be misunderstood and marginalised.

An old Yiddish proverb sums it up in a chuckling couplet:

> When chimney-sweep and baker fight,
> Baker turns black and sweep turns white.

Mimetic conflict, the mutual imitation of two opponents who replicate each other's gestures of aggression with an almost balletic symmetry, ensures that human beings will often derive their deepest identity, their sense of ultimate self, from their rivals and not from their role models. It is the enemy who names us. The Church of Ireland was low so long as the Roman Catholic Church in this country was high. My Redmondite and Republican ancestors detested each other, although their life-style as the Johnny Come Latelies of the new confessional statelet was utterly indistinguishable in every respect. It is the other, then, who brings us into the world. Despising others is deeply energising. Someone said recently that exposing a corrupt politician was as good as first sex. And it's true. Witch-finding, as I know abundantly from my own life, brings with it great psycho-sexual gratification. I've never felt more stable or sane. Likewise, the demise of the antagonist can suddenly invalidate our entire raison d'etre, because the point of honour has long since become the starting point of our very being in the world, and we're lost without it. We are so like those we dislike that we become their facsimiles, and we are orphaned of all our originality in the aftermath of their passing. They appear, in the terms of Girard's anthropology, to be stumbling blocks; but in reality they are our cornerstones, and we build our lives upon them.

We are, in a word, addicted to victimage and vendetta. If, like the saints, we try to internalise all our rage, we become infested with introverted, psychosomatic violence. As statute and case law make it harder and harder for any of us, on pain of the most terrible penalties, to exhibit any breach of the peace publicly in our pacific first world social democracies, our entertainment industry, the proxy of our labile pugilism, becomes ever more psychotic on stage, screen and television, as the bread and circuses of bloodshed soar and spiral from one baroque abattoir to another arena of unimaginable virtual lethality. You can't raise your voice in a video shop, but the compensation is that you can rent genocidal extravaganzas. The poor perfidious Jews of my parent's generation were refurbished in my childhood as the perfidious scheming Soviets or the dementedly cruel Teutons only to be repackaged in my daughters' day by the new Satan, the undifferentiated Muslim masses, the rising sea levels of our current caricature, the aboriginal darkness at the mouth of the cave which is no more and no less than the shadow thrown by our own fantastic tribal firelight. We stumble from the sight of ourselves towards one shameful, hateful surrogate after another.

Perhaps that's why Simone Weil maintained that any sentence which begins with the word 'We' is a lie. Because the creation of a community, the provisioning of a We, always depends for its own definition, its own peace of mind, on a borderland, on a beyond-the-beyond where there be monsters, where there be Them that are not Us. Perhaps we need after all the 'hermeneutic of suspicion' that philosopher Paul Ricouer famously recommended to his readers: that's to say, we need the anguish of an agile agnostic impulse, a double agent deep within us, to civilise our profoundest loyalties, to invigilate their self-pity and their self-importance, to keep the lines open at all times between the plurality of the world and our own singular focus.

Lent is the old Anglo-Saxon form of the word for 'length', and it denotes the lengthening of the light as the season of spring gathers its nerve. On Wednesday, Ash Wednesday, many of us will meet in a spirit of reparation and preparation. But the reparation and the preparation won't be gloomy. We won't gather to throw stones at ourselves or at anyone else. We won't gather to self-harm or to scapegoat. Instead, we'll gather to set aside all stones and all stoning: the stone of self-loathing, the stone of resentment, the stone of remorse. We'll come together as friends amounting to family in the recognition that we are agreeable to God and that God adores us. We'll come together in the recognition that whether we believe in God or not, God believes in us. We'll come together in the faith that we are given and forgiven. We believe that we are transformed by a confession of our faith and not deformed by a confession of our sins.

The demoniac called Legion lived all day and all night among the tombs. He would howl and gash himself with stones. That is not what Jesus taught. Let the stone of self-accusation fall from our fists. Vigilantes dragged an adulterous woman out to stone her to death. That is not what Jesus taught. Let the stones thrown at others fall from our open hands. An enormous stone blocked the grave in which the body of Jesus was buried. But God rolled the stone away so that its dead weight would become living light in the body of Christ. Let us now do likewise in the spirit of the Deuteronomic text that tells us, in the wisest jurisprudence on the planet: When everyone is agreed upon the guilt of the accused, let him go at once. You may be sure he is innocent.

Chapter Ten

ATONEMENT

AS A CHILD, I was always afraid of today's reading (Genesis 22) from the Hebrew Bible. Even in my teenage years, I disliked it strongly. The story of the sacrifice of the boy Isaac by his patriarchal father Abraham on Mount Moriah, the future Temple Mount of Zion, struck me as being all together more dismal and sinister than it seemed to the priests of my parish for whom the episode cheerfully prefigured the slaughter of the Son of God on Calvary in my Christian tradition of faith. Calvin, who attended the same school in Paris as Ignatius Loyola, thought the spare and simple account of this homicidal picnic party 'a most memorable narrative', but it made me feel as one awaiting punishment outside the Prefect of Studies' door, more menaced than meek, with gooseflesh prickling my buttocks and a sudden desire to urinate.

I often wonder how youngsters in the third millennium, young males especially, in the other Abrahamic households, Judaism and Islam, respond to the strange, psychoanalytic watermarks of this legend of the inverse Oedipus, the son-killing sire, when they hear their mentors and tormentors in yeshivas and madrasas explicate the narrative of the aborted burnt offering in the traditional theological terms of test and trial, merit and proof, binding and loosing. Isaac, indeed, appears almost as a Christ figure in some rabbinic commentaries and in the work of Josephus: assenting, even quiescent, serenely complicit with the inscrutable will of the Lord through the heart-broken agency of his dad's total semitic submission to God. But for me, Kierkegaard's knight of faith and the expiatory ethos of this prototype Passion was a nightmare, closer in kind to Luther's likening of God's interrogations of us as 'the game of a cat with a mouse, and this is the death of the mouse'. There were years in the college chapel when I only mouthed the words 'Thy will be done' during the Our Father because, Lord's Prayer or no Lord's Prayer, I was terrified that my vigilant, three-headed, mythological God would take me at my word and invade my peace.

Fear, or more precisely, fearfulness, was my commonest emotion when I was small. I was surrounded by fathers and by father figures, each of whom held the keys to my conditional salvation in this world and the next. My own biological father, a reserved and conservative surgeon, provided for a large family by slashing, stabbing and disembowelling his patients on the glittering altar of his operating theatre. We were strictly forbidden even to touch his scintillating arsenal of hacksaws, scalpels and suture needles, but I would steal into his rooms on occasion to study at length the only photographs of naked women that I would encounter until I was fifteen, in the mute and monochrome medical plates of a textbook called *Diseases of the Breast*, its stiff pages sighing in a sort of desolation as I sifted them, shifting from melanomas to mastectomies, from the black barcodes that blotted a patient, elderly face to the miraculous medal hanging around the younger neck of another victim.

The other male presence in my childhood was my good godfather, not only a holy man but a holy fool, the power and prestige of whose office as Chief Justice in the Irish Republic did not for a moment inhibit his redemptive Christian irony as a flawed individual who was modelling his life on the ludicrous example of an executed Jewish criminal. Cearbhall Ó Dálaigh told me a thousand times that the Criminal Justice system is the cultural camouflage of public vengeance and vigilantism; taught me too that its routine reprisals coarsen and contaminate its stake-holding practitioners, that the ligature which links it to Solomonic justice is frequently speculative, and that he himself, a penitent *Príomh Breitheamh*, would answer on the last day to an assembly of recidivists, culprits and casualties whose company the Lord had preferred to that of Pontius Pilate.

Yet I had seen a prisoner plead before him, a baffled, softly spoken, middle-aged man holding up his trousers with his hands because the two escorting wardens who had brought him in manacles from the urinous corridors of Mountjoy Jail had taken his braces from him in order, I imagine, to forestall a bid for freedom, a dash to the door by someone who had for years only seen the tops of double-decker buses over the granite wall. So even my iconic patron, my *patrino*, as lovely and loveable a human being as ever God imagined, belonged, however self-mockingly, to the gospel of violence, to the testament of the fist, to the Torah of reciprocal atrocity.

For that matter, the venerable Jesuit Fathers whose winged soutanes blackened my blinking infancy like the robes of Greek caryatids – for they were in ways more greekjew than jewgreek, more Athenian than Jerusalemite – could loose and bind not only *in seculo seculorum* but throughout eternity. Beyond their anointed hands and the authoritative and authoritarian manumission of the whole medico-legal pantheon, remained the upraised hands of God, hands at once magisterial and maimed, a blessing and a blow in one, instruments of a mystery whose ultimate paternity of all things allowed me, in fact mandated me, without much affection or enthusiasm on my part, to call him Father too. All of this in the thermonuclear superpower stage of a hundred years' war, beginning locally in the Balkans in 1905 and climaxing, after horror upon horror upon holocaust in the recent Cuban crescendo of the world-wide missile crisis. Three successive generations of European fathers since the 1870s had hurled three successive generations of their European sons into the open graveyards of battlefield upon battlefield upon battlefield, until the continent had become a mortuary, and Christendom, beginning in Abba and ending in abbatoir, had consumed itself in a bulimic psychosis of bloodlust and the lost plasma of its age-old gene-pool. 'The old man … slew his son,' as Wilfred Owen wrote, 'And half the seed of Europe one by one.'

No wonder Leonard Cohen, the author of a second psalter, the psalmist of the new and naked millennium, cannot distinguish between vulture and eagle, between massacre and sacrifice, in his song *Story of Isaac*. No wonder the rabbis play darkly with the grammar of Abraham's equivocation when he says to his first-born and his favoured child en route to immolation: 'God will provide the lamb for a burnt offering, my son', for the two things, boy and burnt offering, are indeed one in this appalling parable. No wonder a later pre-Christian telling of the tale, the inter-testamental *Book Of Jubilees*, attributes the filthy suggestion of the test of faith/the will of God to a satanic presence in Paradise, the Prince Mastemah by name, who whispers its beguiling vileness into God's vulnerable ear. That revisiting of the motif rightly identifies the shamefulness of the Lord's sadism in the account in the Book of Genesis, just as an even later Judaic rehearsal of the myth, in the form of a fable or *midrash*, embellishes the scene with angels in floods of tears at the sight of Isaac's fortitude.

Worse, the heresy of a torturing deity persists perversely and pervertedly among us too, for the mind is more ancient than the modernity it flaunts. Most of the time, we go after very strange gods, deathly fetishes we have fashioned from our own haunted innards, gluttonous idols we invoke on the death of children or the birth of bitter personal and public calamity, as if God were not distraught to the point of dementedness by the sight of our sufferings. It is as if we are genetically determined in some aboriginal manner to criminalise and to caricature the nature of

God until its manageable travesty resembles only the failed and daily lineaments of menial human resentment. Sadder still, saddest of all is the degree to which the text of Abraham's examination facilitates the dreadful, discredited theology of atonement in the Christian passion narratives, Saint Anselm's medieval exegesis of the saving mystery of the Cross that has rightly driven so many of my disbelieving generation in disgust both from the Eucharist and from the community, although atonement thinking is only one among many prayerful penetrations of the same blinding theme.

The cultural anthropologists remind us that the myth of Abraham's attempted sacrifice of his son reflects the move from human to animal sacrifice in primitive societies; and the theologian René Girard who began his career as an anthropologist points to a metaphoric instance of the same process in Homer's *Odyssey*, where Ulysses secretes himself under the fleecy belly of a ram to avoid detection by the cannibal Cyclops. There's a ram in the story of Isaac too, but it's not mutton dressed up as Lamb of God. It is an animal whose violence, in a moment of sudden illumination, is seen to be utterly self-defeating – his horns are locked in the undergrowth; his weaponry is out of commission.

Yet the death of the ram is in a sense secondary. The real death that occurs on Mount Moriah is the death of the false god that Abraham has believed in up to this pointless point, the cruel, conscienceless, tyrannising task master of voodoo and the cult of extinction, the totemic god of the hatchet and machete, an imaginary, inhuman god whom we summon and embody whenever we assign our miseries to his mastery and our pain to his pleasure. For the supernatural power that demands death, the death of a defenceless child, the eradication of a future, the abolition of a blessing, the sterility of seed, is, as Girardean exegete Gil Bailie reminds us, called *Elohim* in the text: *Elohim*, which is the plural of *El*, the Hebrew noun that means 'the gods'; whereas the divine presence that intercedes to appeal to the crazy patriarch in his moment of madness in the urgent, rebuking double vocative of the text – 'Abraham, Abraham' – is called Yahweh by the authors: Yahweh the God of Israel, the redeeming, radiant Lord, the Holy One who graciously gifts us at every moment of our living and our dying and our rising again, and whose holy spirit is closer to us than the breath in our body.

At the very beginning of their dialogue, the Lord had said to Abraham: 'Get thee out of thy country, and from thy kindred, and from thy father's house, unto a land that I will show thee.' Now expatriation is a more straightforward manoeuvre, as I know myself, than the relinquishment of family ties; and the loss or the lack of kindred is an easier thing again than the deep abdication of the father's house. To quit the father's house is the hardest command, because the father's house, the cultural haunt – and cultural haunting – of our childhood, has many mansions, most of which are deep within us. Wretched, retaliatory, atrocious, non-biblical gods run amok in the passageways of our earliest memories. They are the *Elohim*, if you will, the pagan pantheon, the poltergeists and pookas who talk the language of God's will and God's way.

Let us set them aside. Let us allow them to leave us. Let us come down from the mountain. Let us abandon fratricide for fraternity, foul play for playfulness. Let us await in utter joy the kind advent of Yahweh.

Chapter Eleven
PARADINGS

I FELL ASLEEP during the television broadcast of the Saint Patrick's Day parade and I dreamt of my parents. In doing so, I had left a forced and a factitious moment of community for a factual, and perhaps even a truthful, one. After all, childhood is the primal commune, the instinctive kibbutz, not necessarily because of happiness or heartbreak, those tantalising identical twins, the Gemini of our singular state, but because habituation is the place of our deepest identity. Beyond sadness or serenity, only our parents are immortal now. Their voices call at closedown to the sheltered housing and the hospices on the medium wave of the deepest human memories, summoning the elderly and the dying into a lasting supper and a long bedtime from their street gangs' games and their back garden hi-jinks, from their homework and their hot water bottles. This remembering of the archaic present is remembrance too, a form of holy communion under both species of our flesh and blood, the eucharist of the brainstem in its final stages. It is anamnesis, the total recall of the Passion and Resurrection of human nature in the person of Christ, and therefore the opposite of amnesia.

Which brings me back to the forced and frowsy make-believe of Paddy's Day, as soulless and dispiriting as the militarised gymnastics in Red Square under the Soviet Union. Leninist-Marxism may have been a particularly spectral, if not ghoulish, form of the Holy Spirit, but it was paracletic in its recognition that loot underlies everything. We will talk about our orgasms but not about our income. You cannot fabricate any form of community that will combine Foxrock and Finglas under the specious sign of a papier-maché patron saint, when the ideology of smash-and-grab has replaced the old order of hit-and-run. The children of privilege, the patrician class in our gluttonous statelet, are more at home in Johannesburg than in Jobstown. They would experience terror beyond any African safari if their armoured jeeps were to break down en route to their holiday homes as they bisect or bypass the discreet ghettoes that encircle our cities, because the majority shareholders no longer have anything in common with their co-nationals or their co-religionists – if indeed any co-religionists remain. The bourgeois parishes in the archdiocese of Dublin are still packing them in, at least for occasions of hatch, match and dispatch, christening shawls, wedding gowns and sports jackets in place of shrouds, but in the disadvantaged districts, where the new begging bowl is the satellite dish of cultural starvation, those who have been refused seats at the feast have walked out on wafers that masquerade as food. They are tired of being conned by the likes of me.

Post Christianity in our country is paralleled by a meagre, modular form of history teaching, all chronicle without chronology, an awful audio-visual pick-and-mix, such that neither national narrative, the religious or the political, exists in legible or learned form in most of those who process in painted bin liners through the boulevards of the capital on the patronal feast day. Truly they are living on scraps while Dives networks timeshares in the vomitorium. For the erasure of the past has as its corollary the erosion of the future into the depthless instantaneity of the foxy politics of the present moment; and only the gigolos of Lady Violence, the paramilitaries turned parliamentarians on all sides, persist in their little, linear hermeneutic of whodunit and who started it. What can the world of the ring fort say to the world of the ring road, the breastplate of Patrick to the formula milk of modernity? The more so, since the feast of the British bishop is itself a politic fiction which, while marked monastically in medieval times, was largely contrived in the eighteenth century by a meliorist English administration that tried to eclipse the somewhat sanguinary Williamite anniversaries by subsidising a less sectarian shindig that could appeal potentially both to papist, protestant and presbyterian.

I should own up at this point to two things. In the first place, much to my initial embarrassment my faith has become more important to me over the years than either nationalism or nationality, the hardy perennials of Irish Lit, Plc, with the result that Patrick's Confession interests me more than the bloodless carnival which commemorates him. In addition, the day that's in it is a major hosting for the Dispersion, and I am not dispersed, at least in the sense – more parochial than provincial, I hope – that I'm a villager born of villagers, themselves the residuary legatees of villagers who have pottered around the same parts of Dublin since Napoleon died on Saint Helena – an island outpost to which, incidentally, the first Cumann na nGaedhael government wanted rather grandiosely to deport its republican incorrigibles during the Civil War.

When I was small, I played at a pond in the middle of a great garden that belonged, I think, to Saint Andrews' College; and half a century later, the descendents of the ducks I disturbed in the days of the Cuban missile crisis revisit the site each summer in their own mild remembrance, their own modest anamnesis, the waddling mallard and his dowdy mate, perplexed by the lack of water outside the windows of the Radio Centre in RTÉ where I work and write as a fifty-year-old man, which is the average life expectancy of the planetary male. Upriver on the Dodder, where my father carried his mother on his back from her flooded home, like Aeneas portering his Pappa out of Troy, and where a psychiatric heron in profound denial stabs at the glint of beer cans and the gleam of umbrella spokes in the fretting current, stands the Church of the Sacred Heart where I have worshipped since infancy, a triumphalist nineteenth-century house of God constructed in atonement for the venial and the venereal sins of the denizens of Donnybrook Fair.

In the strict sense, then, I'm neither exile nor emigrant nor expatriate. I haven't left for ever, which is exility, departure as deportation; nor have I left in the hurting hope of eventual homecoming, which is the salted wound of emigration; nor have I left in the determined expectation of regular return visits, which is the tart medicinal aftertaste in the open mouth of the expat. I haven't fled the jurisdiction for the dominions like my great granduncle who lost his heart to a heretic Protestant with pretensions. I haven't had my tonsils and my anus examined at Ellis Island in New York like my granduncle who spent his savings on a tillage farm that the winds of the Dustbowl blew, grain and grit, into the neighbouring state during the Depression. And I haven't left the country like my own beloved brother who filled his sneakers with topsoil from a potato field in Wicklow before he boarded a plane for starlight in the Southern Hemisphere and the sight of constellations he had never named through the telescope we shared when we were children growing into and out of each other's clothing.

Yet in a larger sense we are all displaced persons. If we are here still, we are here without being still. It isn't simply that the dormitory towns of Dublin, say, are deemed now to be Drogheda, Mullingar, Carlow and Gorey, so that the link between grandparent and grandchild, between the two generations that walk at exactly the same pace in a procession of the gifts which makes the ritual of remembrance possible, has been broken into bits and pieces of bank holidays and text messages; for the family has been in nuclear meltdown for a century. It isn't simply that we have passed into pluralism, for Pentecost is a godsend, and we can lift up the Irish telephone directory these days like the Gospel book at Mass, to acclaim it in song, its A to Z, its Alpha and Omega – Adelugba, Adeniyi, Adeyemo, Adkins, Adler, Adlington, Afe, Advincula, Adye-Curran, Ahern, Ahmed, Aiken, Alexander, Al Azaid, Anon, Anonymous, Another! – though our receptivity would be more refreshing if there weren't a media moratorium on the expression of misgivings. In any event, as secular Europe teeters, senile and sterile, towards Zero Population Growth, the future belongs to egg and sperm, to those who bring life into the world and bring it abundantly, and so this new millennium is the birthright and the birth rate of the next great Western migrations.

There is no stability, vowed or otherwise. There is only the stable and the stable place: steam from the placenta rising like incense off the dirty floor of travail and travel. Even the continents are parting at the speed of fingernails. Yet this tiny planet is the Petri dish of the whole universe in which there is nothing more majestic, be it supernova or subatomic particle, than the human person. The paschal mystery is the metronome of our species, for we are always rising and falling, falling and rising, dying and resurrecting, from conception to crescendo. We may preserve the pictures of our children as tots and toddlers in our wallets and handbags, but they are dying to become adolescents and dying as adolescents to become young adults and dying again as young adults to become parents. The dialectic of our welfare and our farewells confirms us as transients and aliens everywhere in the caravanserai of the body, its gland and cartilage. In our stop-start, get-up-and-go-again incarnations, in our fertile reversals and our dogged, doggone fragility, the mystery of Christ's failure is altogether more interesting than the great good fortune of conventional messiahs, for we are literally metaphors, shifting shapes in search of meanings that will ring out our changes in the anticlockwise tempo of eternity, which is the liberating endurance and duration of time itself.

Patrick, consecrated a bishop in late middle-life and ministering to a small Christian congregation in north-east Ulster, struck west in his old age to the pagan perimeter of the known world, against the protestations of the Roman-British hierarchy who opposed him, and he retrieved there the place of his previous enslavement, the site of his dismal captivity, which is the only location he names in his autobiography, because that was where God had made love to him in the milieu of his loneliness. Imperial Europe had lapsed into a drooling, immobilised Alzheimer's apathy, so forgetful of itself that its roads and its aqueducts would be attributed in time to the genius of space invaders. Patrick himself almost certainly believed that the world was ending. All the more reason to tell the story, to share the food, to pass the Word from person to person: that God is and that God becomes us, that human beings being human is the high point of Creation, and that we are summoned to dance with the wind of God's walkabout like deciduous trees with their arms in the air and their feet in the living ground.

Chapter Twelve
CROSSINGS

TODAY'S GOSPEL (John 3), which includes the exquisite epitome of faith – that 'God so loved the world he gave his only Son' – always reminds me of a neon sign in the foyer of a flea-pit motel in Los Angeles many years ago that read *Strictly No Solicitors*; for it was in such a wall-fallen breeze block, with a revolver at reception and a bedroom porno pay-as-you-view television set which was chained to the skirting board, that a bout of heartburn without antacids kept me awake most of the night reading a Gideon Bible I had found in the empty wardrobe. It was that or female mud wrestling on Channel Three, and my fetishes did not include the mud, which rather ruined the occasion.

Actually, the taciturn night porter had nothing against attorneys. *Strictly No Solicitors* in fact prohibited prostitutes, although an adroit Irish application of the imperative is not implausible. Equally, the ponytailed and tattooed desk clerk wasn't, I suspect, evangelising in Jesus' name. Gideon Bibles are a world wide, white collar initiative amongst low-church Protestant Christians who have a paradoxically sacramental sense of the unescorted strength of the Word of God in black hardback editions, an Augustinian sense, almost, of the 'tolle lege', of the take-and-read.

So I took and read through the small hours, to the beat of the background accompaniment of Motown music in the lobby, horns, hoots, honking, the svelte soprano sound of brakes on burning rubber on the boulevard, the counter-tenor of police sirens, and the agreeable fracas from the ghetto blaster on the other side of the pebble-dash partition where the couple making love in the next room turned out, mid-morning, to be obscenely old, at least thirty-eight or forty.

What remains of that first real meeting with the mesmerizing and mythological language of John 3:16 are the multiple translations of the verse as mantra and mission statement on the slim, translucent cigarette paper of the Bible I was browsing. The same sentence, which is of course a simultaneous acquittal, appeared in a hundred-and-one Indo-European and Oriental tongues in the prefatory material, from Urdu to Arabic, from Roman script to Korean characters, from Greek demotike to Caighdeán Gaelic, in the calligraphy of every continent and culture.

I would go on over the years to encounter the same cherished citation, the same Pentecostal profusion in hostels and hotels, in carpetless pensions and luxury penthouse apartments, in hospital rooms and the suites of sanatoria, in places that sometimes resembled pictures by Edward Hopper and sometimes paintings by Hieronymus Bosch. Indeed, a stolen copy of the Gideon Bible saved my skin in the early 1970s when the sight of it in my student rucksack at Holyhead deflected a British detective who was searching through my soiled Saint Michael laundry for terrorist explosives, although his sniffer dog had already sensed the presence of the costly Lebanese hash – most of which I found, to my later fury, had been adulterated with asparagus by my teenage Piccadilly dealer – that I had proudly secreted in a polythene wraparound on the train from Victoria as proof positive to my varsity friends in Dublin that, so far from being a collar-and-tie freshman, I was in fact a very cool kid.

That's a long time ago, of course, and I've reached new highs in a non-narcotized manner over the last thirty years or so. In the meantime, many of the Gideon Bibles have been included in the bonfire of the books because, in our peculiar, postmodern and politically correct liberal tyranny, they are deemed to be a source of infection in our Health and Safety systems; so the little Johannine line, packed with protein like the pemmican that polar explorers carry with them into the Aurora Borealis, may not be as visible these days as it was when the Fourth Sunday of Lent was known in my childhood as Laetare Sunday, a semi-festal repast half-way through the stomach noises of the fasting season, when the priest behind the bars of the altar rails traded in his mourning purple for a slightly more frisky shade of pink. Yet the same quotation from Saint John's post-resurrection reflection on the meaning of the death of Jesus of Nazareth stays with us as the summons and the summation, the very Summa in fact, of our Judeo-Christian journey.

The gospels agree that you have to lose your life in order to save it. This paradox – for everything in Christianity is pre-eminently paradoxical – extends naturally to your faith as well. You have to lose your faith in order to save it. You have to kill the bogus Buddhas of your nursery and your natal place, of your adolescent reasonableness and your adult rationalisations, in order to create a sufficient space of waste and emptiness for the wind of God to ventilate. You can return to the stories and to the store of food, to the scriptures and to the sacraments, only by relinquishing them, because the sound that may be speech and the speech that may be dialogue carries farthest in desert areas and across the face of the deep. In these parts the sweat of your own exertion will never precipitate as rain. All it can produce is salt water and eventual dehydration. We are not saved by ourselves but from ourselves by the antecedent Otherness of real human community and by the even more previous priority of the redemptive divine communion that is embedded and embodied in our modest, mud-hut solidarities of family or faith when, and only when, those families and those faiths are not satanic structures that practice scapegoating but are instead broken down and broken open in their hospitality. The return on this isn't so much immortal life in the hereafter as it is eternal life in the here and now.

I say this because, in the only theological insight I've ever had, it has come to be clear to me in my own life that Christians are just that: they are Christians and not, as it were, Godians. Christianity has nothing to do with belief in a god. We are not simple theists or even simpler deists. The Supreme Being, the God in whom the American monetary system trusts to the extent of stamping its faith on its coinage is not, as Stanley Hauerwas reminds us, the God of Abraham and Isaac and Jacob and Jesus. He is the God of America against whom, amongst many others, some of them at large and at liberty in our own Irish pantheon, the Commandments warn us so strictly and stringently as being murderous and megalomaniacal idols that abolish the future by consuming our children.

Which is not to say that I don't entertain the fondest affection for the United States. They received me and enraptured me as a witless guest in my student salad days, giving me books to read, thresholds to cross, migrations to stabilise me, plurality to specify me, and, most of all, an experience that began as an exit and ended as an Exodus, a short-cut that matured into the long way round, a passing through that became a personal Passover. Yet I left America and returned to Europe for reasons that have something to do with its religiosity.

Since I was sixteen, I had been conscious of a hairline fracture in my psyche that would be diagnosed in due course as bipolarity. Even before it was recognised as manic depression, I knew that my brain had a mind of its own, that my intellect was not identical with itself as any self-respecting cogito should be, and that it was only a matter of time before some catastrophic disintegration occurred. If this terrible thing were to happen again in delusion and depression, I wanted to protect myself by experiencing any inevitable collapse of consciousness in the Catholic culture of Europe and not in the Protestant civilisation of America, because failure was a ghastly fiasco in the States whereas in Europe failure, even in the most secular states, still signified a personal event replete with meaning, a metaphysical rendezvous where human plight and the pain of God would meet and mingle in a dark night that might also be in some shape or form a mystical vision.

This Christian belief in the fecund efficacy of failure as a chrysalis of human growth, in the recognition of defeat as a fearless feat of the heart, is rooted in the revelations of the Hebrew Bible. In today's reading from the second book of Chronicles the devastation of Temple and territory, when Babylonian power left the Holy City like a blood-soaked sanitary towel, is understood not as cessation but as Sabbath rest, the slow, subliminal renewal of whole and holy entities. And it's interesting, incidentally, from a current Celtic perspective that the disaster to Jewish cult and culture is attributed to a breakdown in the necessary discourse between the double-ministry of priest and prophet, of tradition and critique, of what Catholic Christians nowadays would call the parallel roles of Peter and of Paul.

It's in the cross, however, in the crucial and excruciating obscenity of casual human violence, that God's self-description as a saviour is exposed, like a photographic negative, outside the encampment in the rubbish dump of Calvary, where the memory of the killing of one condemned criminal signifies God's total recall of all humanity, especially of those whom humanity has deemed not to be human at all. So, in the Greek of Saint John, our weak and wounded nature is lifted up to hang and is lifted up to heaven in the same moment by the same verb, for the passion narratives vivisect the beating heart of the violence that we call keeping the peace, law and order, the status quo, social cohesion, self-preservation, public demand, the democratic mandate, the moral imperative. In fact, in last October's survey by the US Pew Research Center, it emerged that 21 per cent of

American Roman Catholics believe torture is 'often' justified, 35 per cent of American Roman Catholics believe torture is 'sometimes' justified, and another 16 per cent of American Roman Catholics believe torture is 'rarely' justified. That means that 72 per cent of American Roman Catholics accept the discretionary use of torture, after two thousand years of reading and re-reading the same comparatively frank and user-friendly accounts of the Passion of the Lord.

Is it any wonder that the word 'kosmos', which is Saint John's habitual expression for our inhabited reality, what Chesterton once called our 'visited planet', the earthen, unearthly world, should be such a sombre term in the fourth Gospel, where the human project is seen as deeply damaged and damaging? Is it any wonder, either, that the two NASA lunar astronauts walking awkwardly on the surface of the moon almost forty years ago should have cried inside their misting helmets at the sight of the beautiful blue ball that was suspended opposite them, the green genesis of where they had come from in the first place, glowing now like a sanctuary lamp or the luminous ultrascan of a foetus in the pitch darkness of outer space. They may not have been born again, those crew-cut scientists in the sea of Tranquillity, but they were in a sense reborn, and reborn 'from above' – which is, paradoxically, what is meant in the conversation between Jesus and Nicodemus in today's reading. For the word *Anóthen* is a textual pun, since it means both 'again', 'a second time', 'anew', 'afresh', but also 'from above'. Nicodemus intends the former, Jesus enlists the latter. It is a moment of mutual rabbinic playfulness. It is also a call to conversion, not to the Now, Now of mere moralism, which is the alias of violence, but to the lucid urgency of the Now of God.

Chapter Thirteen
PALM FOR THE PASSION

WHEN I WAS A CHILD, I always thought that Jesus' entry into Jerusalem happened at the wrong time. More precisely, perhaps I should say that I always regarded it as a curtain raiser for a proper, plenary procession on the other side of Easter. The real *son et lumière,* the authentic *sturm und drang*, should have taken place, I thought, after the Resurrection when the Risen Lord would parachute in out of the blue like a blinding, helmeted American astronaut returning from a lunar landing mission in his shiny armour. Then the whole town would go crazy around him, the crowded avenues suddenly singing and dancing in lip-synch and lock-step, like that marvellous street scene in the musical *Oliver* where the milkmaids and the postmen and the flower-sellers get carried away by the dawn chorus, and the citizens of London are transformed into a troupe of performers, a cast complete with choreography and chorus lines. Not that everybody would be tap dancing as the Son of God strolled into centre-city Zion. Procurator Pilate, Archbishop Caiaphas, Mafia mobster Herod and their lickspittle retinues of bullyboy bodyguards, legionaries and militia men, would be doing the biggest beezers imaginable in their togas and tunics as the Lord vaporised them contemptuously with a cobalt laser flash from his forehead.

This may not be the most edifying exegesis of Jesus' entry into Jerusalem as it's reported variously by the four canonical evangelists, but it does reflect and reveal a representative childhood in the early 1960s. I'd be a grown man by the time I discovered the so-called 'Vengeances', those bloodthirsty medieval miracle plays in which the Resurrected Christ rampages around Palestine, settling scores with anyone who had disbelieved his message of non-violent forgiveness. But I understood from infancy that society was a structured system of penalties and punishments, that justice was the Latin word for getting even, that retaliation is the serious business of the workaday world, and that revenge brings with it a psychosomatic peace of mind that is both satisfying and stimulating.

Whether I was punished at home or at school or on the way to or from one or the other supervised space, I was part of a culture in which the physical force tradition was both socially sanctioned and spiritually sanctifying. One of my granduncles had been a freedom fighter, voting on behalf of his Cork constituency against the ratification of the Treaty in the Dáil debates of 1921, but his prestige in my child's eye was never parliamentary. Rather it was in direct ratio to the banditry I invented for him *ex nihilo* in classroom conversations as an antecedent and an adjunct to the slowly forming myth of myself. A Redmondite relation who had ministered as a chaplain to the uniformed children in no-man's land during the genocide at the Somme had considerably less sex appeal than my poor, put-upon Uncle Seamus. The blood on his hands was not, at the time, sufficiently red-handed and romantic. Nowadays, of course, the reverse would obtain. The back lane of the revolutionary has been secularised and the battlefield of the conscript has been sacralised, because fashions in violence alternate like hemlines. Bloodshed, like the little black number, is always within the vicinity of vogue, so long as it isn't the disgustingly female sort that is always and everywhere taboo in the male refectory.

If the historical Jesus greatly disliked crowd dynamics and the public relations orchestration of the mob, he has never suffered from a shortage of stand-ins. I may have been too young to palpitate over the Beatles at the Carlton cinema, but I saw President John F. Kennedy, cool, charismatic and chaste, slew past a Mathews' honour guard at a walking pace in his open-top motorcade along O'Connell Street in 1963. Barely six months before, in the breathless eyeball-to-eyeball encounter with his Soviet opposite (a man so similar to his Western counterpart, it strikes me now, that their names begin with the same letter), Kennedy had saved my life and those of everybody else in Donnybrook, including our gardener who lived in Dún Laoghaire. Not alone that, but he had saved face as well, which, according to my cultural mentors and tormentors, was of more metaphysical importance than a mere headcount of rescued hostages. Now he was before me in the flesh. He was really present. He was, in fact, a form of the real presence. I could almost reach out and touch him, if not the hem of his robe, the running board of his motor car. Power would pass from him into my person and I would begin to exist in my own right because people would start to respect me. Self-esteem, after all, derives from the esteem in which others hold us. Without those others, there is no self. Their reactions would therefore activate me. I might even go on to such great things that I would excel the President. He might begin as my inaccessible role model but he would end as an extinguished rival. Every man in the world would want to wrestle naked with me in front of the fire until I bit their ear, like the Big Fella, in a rite of brotherhood. Every woman in the world would want me to impregnate them, though I was not yet quite sure of the mechanics of mating and had only ever slept with my guardian angel, a quiet transsexual according to today's nomenclature.

If mixed fortunes merit a mixed metaphor, it could be said that today's sacred cows are tomorrow's fatted calves; or, to use a more generally beloved Palestinian quadruped, today's lamb of

God is tomorrow's black sheep. I didn't realise in 1963 that celebrity begins in cult and ends in culpability. Poor President Kennedy himself would be transformed in short order from a chevalier of Western civilisation to a degenerate sex addict. This trajectory, which is that of any stone or small missile, records an arc of the greatest possible gravity, beginning with a motion upwards and ending with a fall to earth. My younger daughter Lucy would speak of this ballistic process as the hero-to-zero syndrome, and, while she might apply it within the narrow categories of classroom and sports' field, she would not be entirely surprised to discover that the very word 'category' in the Greek language means 'to bring a criminal charge against'. To desire is always the first stage in resentment. It is the noose in its first manifestation as a halo. It is the electric chair in its introductory phase as throne. For the half-rhyme between amity and enmity is no semantic accident.

Commonly we distinguish between Palm Sunday and Passion Week. Even to speak of it as Passion Sunday seems somehow stilted and donnish. It is surely the smiling, south-facing side of the storyline that turns sour only later. I've even seen the provost of a cathedral ride a donkey into the nave of his church to the utter elation of little children in the pews for whom animals are altogether more adorable than a long-haired Logos. But the reality is that the triumphal entry into Jerusalem is an integral part of the Passion narrative, the first stage in the carnival of ridicule and rejection that ends with a naked man defecating on a stake in the city dump. Indeed, the branches of the trees that bestrew the pathway into the sacred precincts are torn from the wood of the cross. It doesn't matter so much whether the gospel texts commemorate an event that occurred during the feast of Tabernacles or Passover. It doesn't matter, either, that Matthew makes a dog's dinner of the scriptural reference underlining the double citation of an ass and a colt. It may not even be earth-shatteringly important to determine how often Jesus actually visited Jerusalem, a tally which engages and enrages the learned in all sorts of probability calculus.

What counts is that the groupies who idolise Jesus will be the gang who anathematise him in a few days' time. The same mouth that shouts 'Hosanna' will cry out 'Crucify'. They are the mob, the 'mobile', the violent, vacillating crowd whose nature, at the point of critical density, will transmute from cricket to locust and from person to primate. In the sonorous Latin term 'turba', from which we derive perturb and perturbation, they are the free-floating, fickle, fascistic mass whose saliva may be drool at one moment and spit at the next. Whose feet they kiss today they will discover tomorrow to have feet of clay. Whom they lionize today they will throw to the lions tomorrow. In contemporary terms, they are the indignant readers of the morning newspapers, whether of the small-print, large-format ones we call broadsheets or the large-print, small-format ones we call tabloids, for we are all bewitched by both forms of witch-finding, and the court of public opinion is par excellence a blood sport that begins with divinising and ends in demonising.

'Behold,' say the religious authorities, 'the whole world has gone after him'; but this, in the Gospel of John where the word for world is always contaminated by violence and disorder, becomes an ironic anticipation of the pursuit, the chase, the cornering, the kill. As a devoutly observant Jew, Jesus would have been endlessly alert to the least suggestion of the social delirium that stretches across a spectrum of uncleanness from infatuation to idolatry, for Judaism is first and foremost the repudiation of human gods. 'If these should hold their peace,' the Lucan Jesus remarks, 'the stones would immediately cry out'; and there is a delicious semidemiquaver of irony in the mention, for truly the just man is always within a stone's throw of the hillbilly multitudes whose hoopla can darken into voodoo at any moment. Nowadays, as Girard reminds us, 'it is the Christians who say: If we had lived in the days of our Jewish fathers, we would not have taken part in shedding the blood of Jesus.' But this is nonsense. We are all cut from the same cloth. The biochemistry of the crowd is always viral. The frenzy of hypnosis will destabilise everyone, even a seven-year-old boy in a balaclava at Nelson's Pillar.

Because the gospel accounts do not close by disclosing the retaliatory symmetries of pure and perfect vengeance in the traditional way, like Odysseus cleansing his mansion of his wife's clients, they institute a new form of narrative, a new form of the perfect ending. There is no grand public finale. Nothing awful happens to any of the baddies. They die, thank God, contentedly in their beds with a clear conscience. For that perfect sphere, the vicious circle, which is also a hermeneutic circle, is dismantled. There's no vendetta, no jihad. Jesus appears as Christ to those who loved him and are broken-hearted. They spread the word. Wounds heal; healing itself is a new kind of woundedness. And the end, because it is open, is interactive. There is death and there is deliverance. The breaking of heads has been replaced by the breaking of bread. There is violence without vindication and there is vindication without violence. Saint Matthew in a cinematic, Cecil B. De Mille style, lavishes earthquakes on the mise-en-scene, but these too belong to a redundant rhetoric. For something in our nature has been quietened at last.

Chapter Fourteen
EASTER MEETS WEST

I LOVE THE EASTER CEREMONIES and I detest the cross. Some part of me, some prudent and prudential dimension of my life, far prefers the Eastern Orthodox emphasis on the imperial Christ, on Christ enthroned and Christ enabled, on the sometimes scowling, sometimes serenely impassive iconic countenance of the Byzantine Godman in those glittering, acoustical apses that someone else's tour guide talks about while we eavesdrop gratis guiltily, feeling a wee bit secular and self-conscious in our sun shorts and tank tops. Even as a youngster, when I should have been home in Donnybrook, Dublin, helping my mother nurse a dying brother in the awful bed-smells of terminal illness, I was off grandly gallivanting on Mount Athos during Holy Week, luxuriating in the little aesthetic after-shocks of the bass line and the baritone line in the coenobitic monastery of Simonas Petra.

On the other hand, Latin Christianity, especially in the last thousand years or so, has never quite let the faithful forget that, behind the sumptuous oratorios and motets, behind the streamlined Roman liturgy of the chanted Mass and behind the zoological fecundity of devotional traditions in the Catholic Church, in the gritty actuality of mortal affliction and historical memory, an individual is tormented, tortured, impaled, loses control of his bowels and his bladder, and dies, in asphyxia, of dehydration and blood loss. I may decide to endow my daughters with designer crosses for their party dresses, but the incorrigible reality is that all suffering, as Thomas Aquinas reminds us, is intrinsically evil, and the evil of capital punishment, which is a religious and a ritual form of public vengeance, violence as liturgy, is particularly appalling. In essence, it is the Black Mass, the Satanic rite, the Eucharist in reversal, cannibalism in place of communion.

For that reason, the kissing of the Cross, which is a cultural habit of veneration on Good Friday, deeply dismays me. I simply cannot do it. I will bow to the cross, as I bow in deference and reverence before the immensity of unrelieved human misery in the world that we have made by choice and not by chance, but I'm damned if I'll trivialise it by kissing it, anymore than I'll kiss the lethal injection, the electric chair, or a canister of Zyklon B shaken into the shower room. Even Jesus prayed that the cup might pass. There is a necrophilia of the cross which disguises and dissimulates its speechless task, a sort of sentimentality that is only cruelty in a complacent mood. For the crucial thing about the cross beam – the 'antenna' as it's called in Latin – is that it constitutes an ineradicable reproach to our models of community, to our cultural institutions and, most of all, to our organised religion, to our agreeable and enjoyable forms of consumer Christianity in their godless and godforsaken modes as mere aesthetic adornment and/or social habit. In effect, the cross is saying: religion is grand, but most of it is religiosity. Whatever is not about the cross is probably double-cross, if not double-Dutch.

The cross, in short, happens outside all of our pleasant parish abracadabra and in isolated contradiction to it. The Orientals, especially the Japanese in the sixteenth century, understood this immediately. Dislike of the sign and symbol of the cross was so profound among them that the opportunistic Jesuit missionary Ricci considered by-passing the Passion all together in his attempts to proselytise the Shinto aristocracy of Shogunate Nippon. He would move in one go from the Galilean ministry to the mystery we call the Resurrection. As the rather fastidious Cicero exclaims famously in his *Pro Rabirico*, 'Even the word for the cross should be kept … out of mind, out of sight, out of earshot.' It is as obnoxious as the sight of those starving children in a charity ad break before the next instalment of *Sex and the City*, which is simply not fair to people who've done a hard day's work and are trying to relax, after gridlock and the day's gauntlet, over a TV dinner with a glass of plonk.

The motif of the mockery of Jesus in the garbage dump outside Jerusalem has an assortment of sneerers and jeerers inviting the poor unfortunate to come down off the cross so that they can then believe in him. Most Christians in their heart of hearts hum the same chorus line. Suffering is speechlessness. To be able to speak of suffering at all is not to be suffering; and not to be suffering is not to understand suffering, because suffering is nothing but itself, here, now, this moment, this minute, this mess, this immediacy without limit, without horizon, the loss that shears us eternally from our past lives, the lack that splits us eternally from our future existence, leaving us alone in an awful, anal zero, in the nothingness between BC and AD, between the horror of conception and the joy of extinction. We are born, as Saint Augustine says, *inter faeces et urinam*, amidst shit and piss, and we would much rather not be, not be, although, alas, the doctrine of the Incarnation grimly and grotesquely insists otherwise.

But it's not just Christians who baulk at embodiment. Indeed, if Christianity is a selective reading of the Hebrew Bible in which the prophets displace the Pentateuch, so Islam is a selective reading of Christianity in which Gnostic theology displaces orthodoxy by insisting that Jesus, the Son of Mary, never actually died at all. So the Passion will always be problematic because we would much rather be lighting incense and singing the antiphonal praises of a majestic deity in the distance than having our noses rubbed endlessly in what really matters to the God of Abraham and Jesus: love of neighbour, love of enemy, forbearance, forgiveness, fraternity, non-violence.

If the accounts of Jesus' death in the four gospels of the Christian canon sacralise human suffering, they also secularise human religiousness. They take the mystique and the mystification out of it, out of all its pretty aesthetic etcetera, returning us to the dirty facts of what we are and what we do to each other, often enough in the very name of morality and right thinking and religion. The disciples James and John wanted, God bless them, to sit at Jesus' left and right hand side in eventual eschatological glory, but it's the two crucified criminals at Skull Place who inherit an entitlement to that cohort. It is not the empty tomb or a messianic ascension that became the graphic identity mark of Christianity but the cross as the camp number, as the revolting tattoo that authenticated the historical misery of those who were drawn to the infant faith in the first century. By the time the ironically-named Christopher Columbus planted a life-size cross beside a life-size gibbet on the shore of the New World as the starkly contrastive binary sign of a twofold economy, one human and the other divine, one juridical and the other decorative, he and Christendom along with him had largely missed the point of the crucifixion. The cross had become a corporate logo, a plus sign. Other methods of execution had long been favoured by the Christian states that arose from Roman remnants, lest the reminiscence occasion any embarrassment to their municipal worthies.

What Christopher couldn't bear about Christ is that the cross *is* the gallows, that the death of Jesus interprets the life of God as one of utter receptivity not only towards human beings but also towards those who have been dehumanised by human beings and even towards those who have been the inhuman agents of that dehumanisation, for, as theologian Jurgen Moltmann emphasises, 'the message of the new righteousness … says that in fact the executioners will not finally triumph over their victims (but) it also says that the victims will not triumph over their executioners.' There shall be no more hecatombs, whether of the innocent or the guilty. According to a Talmudic text, Yahweh, being in the end the strangest god of all, promptly rebukes his archangelic regiments for taking pleasure in the drowning of Pharaoh's forces as the Hebrew people cross the Reed Sea safely, for the victimisers too are his beloved children.

The triumph, if any triumphalism remains, will be that of ethics over metaphysics, of our doings and of our dailiness as the realm of eternal vitality. Not that deeds overwhelm doctrine. Doctrines are themselves profound and powerful historical deeds, whether they be the decalogue at Sinai or the beatitudes in Galilee. But the decision, say, by the Emperor Constantine to prohibit throughout his dominions the future branding of the faces of slaves and criminals because human beings are, after all, made in the image and likeness of God, is one particular, prosaic and pedestrian step in our slow and stupid species' gradual amelioration of the apparently limitless violence we inflict upon one another, and is therefore the incarnational correlative of the high talk at the Council of Nicaea which the same potentate summoned.

We hear a great deal nowadays about the *entente cordial* between faith and culture, about discourse and dialogue between these two metropolitan partners. Vatican II made its peace with modernity and with its own ecclesial skeletons, perhaps a little prematurely, given that only fifteen years had elapsed since Hiroshima and the Holocaust brought a tattered curtain down on Christendom. A little more lamentation when the legates arrived in Rome would not have been inappropriate. But the cross itself refuses to be metabolised. It won't be neutralised in the sanctuary or privatised by solitary spirituality. It remains at large and at liberty, a summons to solidarity with suffering everywhere. Our own suffering will only deepen us if we address the suffering that diminishes others.

For the cross finally evades our polysyllabic negotiations with any cultural peace short of the Kingdom, whether that peace be the Pax Romana or the Pax Americana, or any transient union, whether that union is Soviet or European, because the flags of all such fidelities will always end up as body bags, their slogans as ideology. But the cross persists as the monosyllabic answer par excellence that calls us back and forward to the margins of our own nature and of our own culture, and beyond both into a human hospitality that imitates the goodness of God. Perhaps that's why, as priests commonly observe at this time of year, the turn out on Good Friday can sometimes exceed the numbers who show up on Easter morning. It's not out of disrespect or indifference to themes of risenness. We know what our older brothers and sisters have taught us as they sit in sacred time at the Passover seder. We know that the shepherd of Israel is a God of Exodus and not of exit. If we linger it's from loyalty to an image that lives our changes and changes our lives, a sign and a summation of what it is to be human and what it is to be here.

Chapter Fifteen
UNORTHODOX EASTERS

ON THE FIRST FRIDAY OF EASTERTIDE, I was browsing in a bookstore in the centre of the city when in stepped an Orthodox parish priest in his working canonicals who started to deselect paperbacks from the same shelf I was vetting. He was wearing that rather sweet stove-shaped hat that goes with the gig in much the way that curates in my own childhood church used to sport collapsible birettas in the bad old days before the bad new ones, when the hat was passed from deacon to sub-deacon to acolyte before the introit of the Mass of Trent. I assumed that this eastern cleric must be Greek, though it occurs to me now that he might as easily have been Russian or Romanian.

In any event, my vanity was such that I wanted to salute him using the half-remembered Easter greeting that I had learned in the medieval forests of the Holy Mountain of Athos thirty years ago, when companionable monks who looked like dotty hobbits on donkey-back would call out to me as they trotted past the sandals swinging from my rucksack, 'Christos anestin!', 'Christ is Risen!', and I would respond 'Nai, Christos anestin, timén patér!', which means 'Yes, Christ is risen, reverend father!', attaching the title not because the ponytailed greybeard was necessarily ordained, but because it's always a good idea to promote the guard to sergeant in a roadside rekky. Then the kind individual would point me in the direction of the next monastery before asking delicately for a Papastratos cigarette to shorten his route. In Greece at the time, cigarettes,

God bless them, were used as a metric measurement of walking distance. 'Ena cigarou dromo meta podia', 'One cigarette away from here on shank's mare', signified a ten minute hike at most.

By the time I'd thought of the right expression in demotiké and rehearsed it a few times mentally in order not to make a complete fool of myself, the priest was gone. This is, alas, the story of my life and indeed the life of many of the stories I've written over the years. I am always a nanosecond too late with the apt riposte. Belatedness, not the photo finish of swift spontaneity, is my forte, which may help to interpret why I spent this quarter-hour one week ago on Easter Sunday riddling the enigma of Good Friday.

Then the penny, or the drachma, dropped. It was just as well, after all, I hadn't bothered the Pappas – for that is what Greek parishioners call their priests in an ancient and affectionate word, really a primitive plosive that most toddlers on the planet can perform at ten months or a year, and which occurs as far back as Book Two of the *Odyssey* itself, when the white-elbowed Princess Nausicaa tries to lure her father King Alcinous into letting her have the car, or the chariot, for the evening, by calling him 'Pappa phil', 'Dear Daddy', instead of 'Your Majesty'.

What I'd forgotten in my rush to impress a complete stranger with my command of a foreign phrase was that my Orthodox confrere in the bookstore was actually observing the fast of Good Friday while I was being facetiously friendly in the week following the Latin Easter. Rome this year is seven days ahead of the rivalrous liturgical calendar in the city that was once called Constantinople. You can't really enthuse about the resurrection of the risen Lord on the day that commemorates the stench of his brutalised cadaver. You can't traipse through a decade of the Rosary in the candle-lit mortuary chapel, crying out, as a little boy I knew of used to do, 'Easter eggs, Christ is risen! Easter eggs, Christ is risen!'

For Jesus is not up and about on Good Friday. He is not simply dead to the world in a pietistic trance that recommends suffering as a sublime spiritual régime. He is dead, period; and, in the clammy, claustrophobic, paratactic clause inserted into the Christian creed in the fourth century, he is descended into hell. He is not only dead in the stink of quick decomposition in a hot climate, but, even worse, he is disgraced, like a bogus, big-time televangelist exposed as a paedophile, a Bogey man with psychotic pretensions. Carl Gustav Jung may remind us that anyone who can fall so low must have depth; but how does one speak either of rising or of raising when human catastrophe eclipses us, and the loved one or the loved thing, a person or a project – a child, a relationship, a home, a way of life, a life itself – begins to exude the terrible mortal odour of cold plum pudding that a corpse gives off on the second day, regardless of garlands, and we know that we are irretrievably separated from the source of our own sanity in this partial-birth abortion of a world?

In the Passion narrative of the book of Mark, the tormented Jesus can no longer call his Creator 'Father' or 'Abba' – a word I heard again on a Sky News bulletin during Holy Week as a stunned Israeli infant cried out for his parent in the aftermath of a suicide strike in Tel Aviv. Instead, and for the first and only time in the whole of Mark's gospel, the Galilean prophet exclaims 'My God, my God', because the personal preternatural presence who has always accompanied him is now experienced only as an assertion of intellectual conviction in an act of final will.

I may have realised this for the first time on the day my sister married in the giddy, glamrock revelry of the early 70s, all magic mushrooms and mushroom clouds. My brother John, her senior by a few years and mine by many, was being operated on in the old neurosurgical theatre at the Richmond Hospital in north inner Dublin; and my Dad had to alternate all day between gaiety and grief, between witticism and wisecracks at the bridal breakfast and *sotto voce* telephone updates in a soundproofed hotel booth on the root work of the brain tumour that was spreading, like a plant in need of potting, under the cracked and shaven curvature of the skull of his first-born son on the far side of the river. Flowergirls blew bubbles through paper straws in 7-Up in their stem glasses and men in morning coats posed for Polaroid pictures as I told my father, with all the sensitivity of a seventeen-year-old, that the show had to go on.

'Yes,' he said, 'but not the side shows. The side shows are over for ever.'

The fullness of time can be a very empty space. I thought nothing of that exchange for over ten years, until I found myself in a place where I had lost myself, in the closed ward of a psychiatric hospital where strange dressing gowns chain-smoked in the shadows, and nurses with earrings patrolled the carpeted corridors with hostess trolleys full of tinkling Greek and Latin painkillers. I had been there a long time. From the big bullet-proof windows I had seen blossom the colour of snow on the branches of trees and I had seen snow the colour of blossom on the bare ground beneath them; and, in between the two times, where a queue of callipered saplings stood beside a tennis court without a tennis net, I had seen women walking in camel-haired coats through fallen leaves in the autumn, and the same women walking in short-sleeve blouses and canvas espadrilles among green tennis balls in the summer.

One of these women was my wife. She was my wife and she had a child. She had a timid female infant who made strange with me on her weekend visits and who far preferred the chaplain's budgie with its pretty pastel colours and its crackly cackle to the speechless, strongly smelling man in the nightshirt who could not lift his eyes from his hands, who could not lift his hands from his lap, who could not persuade anyone in the whole hospital that his life should be ended by execution because he disgusted the Creation and should be defecated from the domain of being. In fact, he was not a human being at all. He was only a human body.

One day in the closed ward this man had overheard a voice on the wireless that was talking about the beauty of faith or perhaps it was faith in beauty. Perhaps it was both. Perhaps it was about faith and beauty. One way or the other, it was all evergreen Eastern nonsense in a dead, deciduous world. It was all karaoke from lightweight and light-headed inexpensive paperbacks that other people had written because they had nothing better to do with their time. But the voice of the man on the wireless was not entirely unfamiliar to the chain-smoking man in the nightshirt. It reminded him, in its slightness and silliness and shallowness, of something other than itself and larger than itself, in the way in which the cry of a gull in the centre of the city can remind you of the silence of the sea that you have not been aware of for years although you have been within its tremendous vicinity all your life. So the sound of the voice on the wireless reminded him of someone.

Then, when the programme on the radio ended, the presenter's name was given, and it was the same name as the name of the chain-smoking man in the nightshirt in the closed ward.

Church bells are not used to tell the time in the monasteries on Mount Athos. Instead, a monk wanders around the precincts of such places, striking a wooden plank with a small hammer, to remind his brethren that the hammer-blows of Calvary are the metronome of the world. We must find a way of talking about Easter Sunday in a language that speaks to our unspeakable and unspoken Good Fridays, much as a Spaniard and an Italian can understand each other in the radiant Latin flood plain of their shared sources. Then we must find a way of talking about Good Friday in a language that is intelligible to Easter morning, much as an Italian and a Spaniard can inhabit the same reciprocal silences. In the fullness of time, we may even discover that the two events are the one experience, and that the temporal order in which we relate them arises from the fact that we can only imagine eternity, which is the love of God and the God of love, in terms of a table of tenses, in terms of a story.

Doubting Thomas understands this very well. Ordinary folk want their loved ones to return as they were before crisis and stasis beset them, before illness, injury and dying disfigured them. We want the Resurrection without the crucifixion. If there must be a Passion, let it be a most dispassionate one, neither passionate nor compassionate but a passing phase. But for Thomas the paradoxical proof of the Resurrection *is* the crucifixion. Risenness is all hoax, hocus-pocus and hallucination, a kiddies' pop-up picture book, unless and until it informs and transforms every detail and dimension of our falling and rising, our rising and falling.

Early Christians had little difficulty in discriminating the divine ethos of the Christ. It was the humanity of Jesus that they doubted. Today we live in a reverse scenario. But the Christian abides in the hyphen between God's hospitality and the homelessness of humans. For us Jesus is the sign that we are all in God's hands and that those hands carry the marks of our mutilation, like the inked mnemonic of a telephone number on the flat of a mother's palm.

Chapter Sixteen
EMMAUS

EASTER FALLS in the spring. The observation belongs to meteorology, but it has moral and metaphoric consequences too. If the determination of the date of the double festival of Passover links it to the first full moon after the spring equinox, the Church liturgical calendar also connects to a verifiable death in the vicinity of Jerusalem around the time of the Paschal meal in the early decades of the first common century two thousand very odd years ago. So the demise of Jesus occurs in a context of flowering and flourishing and proliferation, just as the largely legendary celebration of Christmas was timetabled to coincide with the sterile depth of the winter solstice. Accordingly, we can see our breath condensing, the word assuming steam if not flesh, when we sing *Silent Night* at the noisiest point in the year, as the birth of a baby boy emits the tiny din of life in the deadened world; and we can carry a newborn lamb to the altar in the months of mucous membrane and the life cycle, although the frisky fellow struggling in my arms ten years ago urinated all over my new linen jacket to the great gratification of the little altar girl who was leading us up the aisle behind the vigil candle, reminding me forever afterwards that the smells of piss and chrism should be close cousins.

This is all anecdotal until we recall that our upside-down friends and family in Australia, say, commemorate Christmas in Fahrenheit 110 and Easter in the temperate banality of their civil winter. As a result, climate contradicts the vulnerability of the

Incarnation and confounds the fragile, far-seeing paradox at the heart of the Passion. Can cultural texts survive the removal of their natural contexts? Can the pain and possibility of birth and death be heard in their own enabling acoustic if the background be groundless? And what, in the case of the Christian Triduum, has the third day to do with the third hour, the Friday fast with the Sunday feast?

Luke's account of the journey to Emmaus (24:13-35) recapitulates the problem in narrative form, for the day trip it describes is also a night crossing. In a theological parable which is probably closer to the several stages of a therapeutic procedure than to any historical occurrence in the afternoon of Easter day, two persons in profound grief – one named, one unnamed in a scriptural invitation to identify ourselves with the incognito – are walking in the opposite direction to the holy city, away from Jerusalem, from a religious epicentre that has become the dead centre of a nuclear implosion, abolishing all point and purpose. They are decentred and they are centrifugal. 'Man is in love and loves what vanishes. What more is there to say?' writes W.B. Yeats; and the dreadfully wounded duo in the Lucan story have loved the ephemeral as humans wantonly will do, for the smile of detachment on the face of the Buddha is a philosophical profile sweethearts cannot easily manage or mastermind, unless it be Chekhov's 'smiling through their tears', the playwright's favourite stage direction in his tragically comical theatre of operations.

So the two men veer towards the periphery in a fragile, far-flung communion of utter bereavement, a fellowship called a 'homilia', from which the replenished Church, post-Vatican II, would derive the term 'homily' as a substitute for the compromised 'sermon'; and in their homilia these men are reasoning – and rationalising – the scandal of loss. The body of the man whom they loved, the model whom they followed, has been disappeared in the tactical subtraction of the social and political violence that safeguards public order, and there is no habeas corpus to call on. The desolate and disillusioned disciples are in freefall. Once they had been en route and on the Way, the pilgrims of a head-spinning walkabout. Now they're pedestrians, their steps an interrupted stumbling. Once they were footloose. Now they're footsore. When a complete stranger crosses their path and asks them what's up, their resentment of his ignorance of their suffering, of a passer-by who has bypassed their plight altogether, defines the rage of each and every person who's discovered, as Seamus Heaney remarks in a recent poem, that 'the human condition is private', that the mystery of our lives is out of earshot in the deaf-mute midst of convivial daily life. Replies Cleopas to the alien other whom he immediately excludes and victimises: 'Are you the only person in the place who doesn't know what's happened?'

Again, in an apostolate of close listening, the strange, estranging presence who accompanies them prompts a fuller divulgence. 'What has happened?' It is a question to them and not an answer from him. For, as my lifelong friend Michael Paul Gallagher once reminded me, Holy Saturday is the Sabbath space, when God does not appear to be working in any way at all, when the chatter of Easter is both premature and immature, and the albs in which we vest are the white flags of utter abasement, bloodstained shrouds and dirty bandages. And this Sabbath does not reach from one sunset to the next sunset only, but from solar eclipse to solar eclipse, from cosmic darkness to cosmic darkness. It cannot be cancelled, it cannot be choreographed. It is all Kyrie and no Gloria. In this endless aftermath, this posthumous no-place, comfort is impertinence, all speech is speechifying.

In the fullness of time and only in the fullness of time, out of the thirst and uterus of our speechlessness comes the first draft of the nightmare. Both bloodied men on the road to Emmaus have stored the tale. Now they tell the story, without the censorship or curfew of later decorum, and their rapid-fire rendition, all loss and lamentation, is the word-perfect verdict of most selves in most societies most of the time: that bread and wine have ended in bread and circuses and in bread and water, that hope and history do not rhyme, although they may alliterate meretriciously to provide a suitable soundbite on Commencement days for mild-mannered militaristic parliamentarians and those resplendent princes of the Church whose speeches are more keynote than keystone. The trust of the two persons on the path to Emmaus has been broken and they cannot yet trust in that brokenness as the fractured aperture of a possible future.

Thirty years ago in California I attended AA meetings with a friend who was in the great and gifted difficulty of personal crisis. Anonymous men and women, strangers on Christian name terms, sat on miniature chairs in a kindergarten classroom among bright acrylic images of talking pigs and pink elephants, under the shadowless overhead lighting of the elementary education system. A freckled sophomore had lost an adored father to the accidental, unintended, inadvertent discharge of a gun in a garden shed, and the report of the shot whiplashed endlessly through her waking hours. A tenured teacher in the faculty ghetto had gone abroad to a dry Islamic state to beat the booze but was bleeding from his bottom from an alchemical blend of aftershave and cigarette-lighter fuel. The midlife mother of a child with Down's syndrome couldn't bear the sidelong glances of the shopping mall that reproached her age and the absence of sensible amniocentesis. Persons with broken hearts and broken minds envied those with broken bodies for cripples and thalidomides at least exhibited the dignity of public stigmata, of sanctified scar tissue, instead of the weeping wounds that gummed the fabric of bright Benetton blouses. How could they redeem their damaged wedding dresses as communion robes, their ripped communion robes as christening shawls?

Who would safeguard the last iota of their pain like the seventh-century pontiffs in Mary Major, Rome, where the fraction of the bread occurred in little linen pouches lest any particle or speck of the body of Christ slip out of sight?

Now the stranger speaks. The other is present. In the parable in Luke's gospel, the distance between the place of horror and the place of healing, between Jerusalem and the general direction of Emmaus is a matter of hectares, roods and perches; and the proof texts of the Passion are pursued programmatically – some clear and some coerced and some incredible – in the books of the Hebrew Bible, because this is precisely how the shocked Christian Jews in Jesus' retinue made slow, eventual sense of the shame of their leader's last days. But the transformative quickening that turns our slow hearts into burning hearts may not happen in the hours of daylight or of darkness but of both over years and decades and the deep duration and endurance of time. The trek is itself the tutorial. It is a seminar on shank's mare, and it consists in our painful, painstaking openness to an altered way, to the way of alterity, not to the closure of one commentary but to the disclosures of an ongoing dialogue, not to a scheduled analysis but to the Greek original of the word, which is 'analusis', a setting free, a releasing, or, in its prettiest, nautical application, a weighing of anchors, a slipping of moorings, a setting sail again.

It is this freshening breeze, this slipstream of the Spirit of God, which lifts and lightens and enlightens the mourning parties in Luke's epitome. Cognition has taken them as far as cognition can go. Now recognition begins and the alias of Jesus is the incognito of the other person they have encountered on their journey. It is evening. In the Jewish ordering of the hours, a new day is about to begin. Their previous destination has been reconfigured as a point of departure. Abide with us, they say. The other has restored the self to itself as only the other can. The stranger has become a guest, the chance comrade on the road a chosen companion at the table.

So the dispersed congregate. The dismembered remember. They take nourishment again. They are eating together for the first time in ages. It is a meal. It is a memorial meal which is both fast and feast. It is a meeting in honour of a host who encounters our hunger and thirst as food and drink, as welfare and refreshment. Much has been sacrificed yet nothing has been lost. Instead, in the long protocols of patience and waiting, everything has been made sacred. Whole-hearted community rises up into holy communion, the holy communion of board and bed, of agape and eros, of relationship and intimacy. The wood of the cross can be sanded and shaped now into the timber of a crib. Good Friday has fallen, as it can and does, precariously and powerfully on the Feast of the Annunciation, just as the very last words in Saint Mark's book, the words 'and they were afraid because', impel us to return to the proclamatory cadences of the very first words of the gospel, sixteen chapters earlier in the text, to go back and forward into Galilee again, to go back and forward to the frank beginning of the Good News of Jesus Christ, Son of God.

Chapter Seventeen
THESE ARE OUR BODIES

EASTER IS USUALLY THOUGHT OF only in terms of the life of the spirit in the hereafter, which is a tremendous pity as well as being theological nonsense, since the story of the Resurrection is equally, if not more so, about the life of the body in the here and now. Most people, Christians included, cannot tolerate the doggedly three-dimensional nature of the event of the empty tomb and prefer to invoke it as a depthless stage setting in a guardedly genteel way at low-key funeral services by way of solemn small talk to buck up the afflicted immediate family until such time as they can recover their morale and get on with life in the transitory universe. Easter, the fabled land of the really rising sun, is well on its way to being seen, like that star in the East which Matthew reports in his Nativity narrative, as being both implausibly pretty and pretty implausible. Just as one might sometimes imagine that the Muslims among us are the only ones left who really believe in the virgin birth of Jesus, so increasingly it's the counter-cultural community who hold the torch for eternal life.

Even worse, many of the supposedly orthodox Christians who do subscribe to the Easter story still spiritualize it to the point where the human person, being regarded essentially as a flitting spirit, a pilgrim soul in transit, is stripped of her magnanimous flesh and blood, her incarnational presence. The abused, anonymous body thereby becomes, perversely, immaterial, its historicity effaced. Cremation, the freeing of the spirit from the vice of flesh-and-blood, replaces burial as the birthing of the future in the passage of the seed. Likewise, the Word assuming flesh becomes an assumption that sensible folk simply don't flesh out. That, we're told, is a Johannine idiom, a mere metaphor, as if metaphor and metamorphosis weren't the most basic cosmic processes in the whole of Creation, as if we human beings in our endless physical and metaphysical transmutations weren't, in the most literal manner, metaphors or shape-changers ourselves, the daily dynamic activity of God's providence.

Well, I believe that the Word assumed flesh – or, as a child once said from a church lectern at Christmas, 'the Word became fresh and dwelled among us' – and that the body is the frisky chasuble of our ordinary priesthood, for, as Chesterton insisted, Christianity is the most materialist religion on earth. 'It was necessary,' that practical mystic Gregory of Nazianzus reminds us, 'for men and women to be sanctified by the humanity of God'; and the best part of the Catholic Christianity that has grown me over the last half-century has been proclaiming this cornerstone creed for two thousand years, whether from pulpit or from priest-hole, singing the psalm of the bodily alongside the praise of the spiritual, against the disgusted Gnostics of every age – many of them, be it said, fifth columnists from within the community – who prefer ether to sweat, atomisers to odours, and sterility to mucous membrane.

Fear of death habitually poses as love of life. It did so during the Pax Penicillin of the 1960s when the commodification of instinct masqueraded as personal freedom, for licence is only loathing in a brighter mood, just as prudishness is only prurience on holiday. Those in the early era of the Church who denied the empirical reality of the crucified body of Jesus, replacing its factual and actual state with a clever conjuror's apparitions, detested as well the physicality of detail in the reportage of the Resurrection, because its particularity champions the profundity of our individual wounded embodiment; and the aseptic sceptics continue their puritan prosecution of our proper nature, its damaged, ageing dignities even now; but the high places and the holy places of contemporary Gnosticism are the gym, the solarium, the sauna, the cosmetic surgeon's operating theatre, the whole, unwholesome pharmaceutical alchemy that seeks to neutralise the creativity of time by preferring an antibiotic perfection to a temporal completeness.

Not that my own religious tradition which is Roman Catholicism wasn't complicit with the culture of inhibition and prohibition against which we are still reacting, however theatrically, today. In a twofold sense, the privy nature of the body puzzled my childhood. As late as Confirmation class in my prep school, I imagined vaguely that a man would dream of his future sons at night, that the woman lying beside him would wake at this and drink the tears that dribbled from his eyes as they filled with affection, and that his glistening serum in her stomach would start to glow like a lightbulb until, in the fullness of time, she passed a baby. The shyness of our state was such that my godmother used to wear kitchen gloves when she washed me in the bath, and I would cover my nipples with my hands out of maiden modesty as she did so, waiting until she went to inspect my magnified fingerprints in the green water through the face mask of a heavily breathing snorkel from the South of France. My first erections when, in the radiant phrase of Anaïs Nin, the 'insolent baton' surfaced, swerved between thrill and terror, for the creature that stretched across my belly, as if sunning itself, was as foreign to me as a lizard.

Puberty transformed my nudity into nakedness, as puberty must, and of course I blamed the bother of it on the benefit of clergy, as the dreary Irish always do; but my student years in California showed me that, for all its breadth and biodiversity, sexuality in San Francisco was as problematical and imperfect as back home in the archdiocese of Dublin, because the work of the body is human and historical and not as sanitised and abstract as pornography would pretend in that odourless utopia where there is neither prolapse nor stretch mark nor battle scar, neither menstrual blood nor bloodshed nor the shedding of saltwater tears and the baptismal waters of bodily fluids. For the truth is, it takes a lifetime to assume flesh, not the three trimesters in the uterus alone but the three trimesters of human endeavour in the world, youth, middle life and old age together.

You cannot love the body of Christ without first cherishing the crisis of the body in all its ages and stages, arisen in time and raised up to eternity, an archangelic hybrid of cherubim and chimpanzee, an alimentary mystery of mouth and anus, of toilet and tabernacle. Only then, through practice and patience, can we recognise our own flesh as sacred scripture. Only then can we incorporate the Song of Songs in our holiest writings, not in the accustomed Cistercian style as an allegorical extravaganza about Christ and his bridal Church but as the plainspoken transcript of our ordinary longings and belongings. For Judeo-Christianity exalted the body until it bore witness to the whole world that the human form is the norm of western art. The transformation of a graveyard into a garden, of mortality into timeliness, in Saint John's account of the Resurrection posits an Edenic renaissance of the spitting image of God. For if the body is the temple of the Holy Spirit, it is not a Greek temple, all clarity and proportion, but a Hebrew tent of meeting, a magnificent mobile canvas makeshift in the sand dunes of infinite space.

To be sure, postmodernity is impatient of high humanism and chastised it rightly if not righteously at the millennium, but the bias which sees our species as a benediction is in our bone marrow and our bloodstream. My first-born daughter told me when she was four or five that she remembered being in the womb, and that she had to keep her eyes closed tightly at all times because it was so bright. So too, in the enabling and disabled plenitude of planet Earth, the gift of life illuminates even the dustmites in our bed linen and the bacteria in our stomachs. Chivalric and amphibious, they are the unicorns and the mermaids of the molecular order. They too shout out inaudibly in the Great Amen of all meaning.

Once I lived in a house on a hill. The window of my bedroom looked out over the lights of a city. Late one evening, when the night sky was as starry as the runways of an airport seen from the porthole of an aeroplane beginning its descent, I watched my wife come in from the car with a bale of little disposable diapers for a new baby and a carton of large disposable diapers for her dying mother in the bedroom beside the nursery. Her breath among the barbed sticks in the barrels at the front door rose up into the air like white smoke. Below and beyond her, couples in the dim dormitory streets of the estates that reached to the horizon were undressing for bed. Women would be reaching behind them to open the clasp of their bras in that backward, bird's-wing motion of the elbows men are so moved by. Husbands and housemates would be lying naked on their duvets and their eiderdowns, with the stigmata of digital watches on their washed wrists and the stencils of socks on their poor, pale ankles, on their kissable Achilles' heels. The night prayer of the body was about to utter itself all over Ireland. From Mizen Head to Malin Head, from Carnsore Point to wherever it is they talk about when they talk about wind and wave and the rain of God and the sun shining through cloud, the compline of the love-act, the eucharist of flesh, was starting in stillness, saying, in the language of touch and tenderness, 'Lord, open our lips, and we shall proclaim your praise'. And the Holy Ghost came down in the form of a pigeon among the vestments on the washing lines.

This isn't to be po-faced about the poetry of the body. Much of its work is in prose volumes. Far from the hard Nordic configurations of the airbrushed photographs in the men's magazines and the women's magazines, which are only the wet dreams of revulsion and the race laws, the reality of sex is infinitely more interesting than the sexualisation of reality by the copywriters and the advertisers. Leaky, fragile, and less than fragrant, sex in the city is no small-screen series. It is graced Greek drama, as complex as consciousness. It is a beatitude, and a beatitude in the older translation. Nowadays we speak of the poor in spirit and the pure in heart as being 'happy', but the Church of my childhood was wiser in its choice of 'blessed'. 'Happy', after all, has a facile inflection, while 'blessed' indicates sanctification but also suffering, for the Anglo-Norman 'blesser', as in modern French, means 'to wound'. It is the blend of woundedness and wellbeing, of injury and rapture, that the body maps, no atlas of a landscape that lies elsewhere but its own good globe, a graciousness that grows on us.

Chapter Eighteen
MARY

THE MIDDLE GROUND in which I have an interest amounting to affection can feel at times like the middle distance, a kind of no man's land. Once you could tell the margins from the mainstream, the edge from the epicentre, but the contemporary landscape in this country is molten, volatile, vulnerable. Sometimes in the dust clouds and the debris it's hard to tell scaffolding from ruins and site-clearance from demolition. For that matter, even the scenic and suburban grounds in which I earn my bread from day to day are a seismic complex, part fault line, part fertile crescent, a cross between real estate (after all this is Dublin 4) and fourth estate (this is also Donnybrook, the American term for a frank and forthright exchange of views). The radio centre in which I've been employed for almost all my working life is, for better and for worse, for richer and for poorer, one important part of a new postmodern national seminary, the virtual Maynooth, if you like, of the print and electronic media. Its orthodoxy, insofar as it has one, includes the vigilant interrogation of the very idea of correct doctrine. We are living in a polity that has shot from a truncated sectarian statelet to a post-religious continental federation in less than fifty years without ever quite attaining the sedimentary self-assurance of the nineteenth century status known as secular nationhood. Once we were a pilgrim people. Now we're the general public. It can feel funny.

Since I was small, watching the metal mast at Montrose rise higher and higher into the sky over the infuriated heads of the householders of Ailesbury Road, who regarded its erection as an industrial eyesore in a paradisal bourgeois preserve, the national broadcaster has been both describing and devising, both enabling and embodying, cultural movement countrywide, migrations of every kind. It's appropriate then that one such thematic momentum in my lifetime – the rapid dismantlement of the Marian cult in a single sorrowful decade – should be signified to my left and right hand side as I look out the office window on a bountiful May evening, the month traditionally attributed to the fourteen-year-old single mother who gave birth in a barn to a child who would grow up to be hanged.

Out there, in a circular chapel of broadleaf trees that refresh and replenish the bleached retina, stands – or, at any rate, kneels – a modern Madonna of the woodland in the form of a naked female in prayerful posture, beseeching and bespeaking the fecund universe, Natura naturans, as they used to say. She is made from vulcanised pine cones by an artist who has opted for the subtle vanity of the anonymity beloved of the great medieval masters and mistresses. The sight of her sculpture fills me with happiness daily as I trot to and from the station canteen. In fact, I have often wanted to pour a libation in her honour, decanting a Styrofoam cup of cool white wine over her high bronzed forehead, but I've always been afraid it'll result in a rust like a rash and land me in trouble with Human Resources.

A few hundred yards in the opposite direction, heading due north towards the heronry in the Dodder, an older, dilapidated image of the Virgin stands in a damp evergreen enclave, a slender stone statue on – am I right in remembering? – a squashed stone snake, in the short-cut gardens of Donnybrook parish, where four generations of my biological family have been christened, chrismed, communicated, and finally coffined. I suppose it's only a matter of time before some Human Rights for

All Reptiles Association will campaign for the removal of this remnant of my infancy on the basis that a plinth with a pulverised serpent demonises the otherness of adders. But I used to pray – or at least to say a prayer there – on my way to the village for the good groceries that my mother called messages back then; and I would sometimes leave wildflowers that might have been weeds at the cemented feet of the Galilean girl during a troubled puberty that ranged mopingly between the loneliness of supervised discos and the sonorous oral pleasures of the rosary. Its mysteries and its mantras brought to mind the night vigil of Ignatius at Montserrat and the drone of native speakers from the West of Ireland who died in Union blue with General Custer at the Little Big Top.

Not that my love of Mary was merely psychosexual, a simple Irish stage if not the simplistic stage-Irishry of a ludicrous literary stereotype meretricious writers traded in until the dreadful death of Ann Lovett at a sub-zero sanctuary twenty years ago finally disqualified all such infantilism. It was grounded instead in the personal knowledge of a whole entourage of concierges and cooks, nannies and nursemaids, in the cut-throat middle class marketplace of Whitaker's Republic. My father knew that the mythical mother of Mary was called Ann only because the New Testament's Magnificat had been cogged by the evangelist Luke from the psalm of Hannah in the Hebrew Bible; and my mother would have understood the new emphasis on her example of robust discipleship in the adjusted Marian leaflet-literature of post-Vatican II. But the real Maries of my childhood and my coming of age were the disadvantaged liminal women who had brought me to the crib and shown me, in the dim community of their coping, what actual human placenta looks like under starlight and the steam of animals in the outhouses of the prosperous and the powerful.

Doggedly gaberdined, many of these teenagers and twenty-somethings came from convent orphanages where orders of decent nuns had raised them in the scarcity of the war years for lives of service, stewarding other women's offspring without badge of honour or benefit of title. Their Christian names sufficed to represent them throughout the parish. If need arose, they could be identified more plentifully by the patronymic of their employer. Some were parentless, some were passion fruit in a puritan culture. Few of them wore lipstick, as if in reparation, unlike the scented ladies at their glacial dressing tables in the bay windows above the pantries, because sexual politics is the perennial poor relation of class distinction and material happiness will always harden its affluent casualties. Only a few days ago I heard a South Dublin memsahib talk about the questionable domestic habits of her Romanian woman.

Now the surrogates downstairs in the distant 1960s said 'amn't' and not 'aren't', until the very word, which stands for 'loving' in the Latin language, became their radiant legend. Their domain would be the kitchen and the bedroom at the top of the house, and the children for whom they were both an ecosystem and the earth itself, waited impatiently for their parents' social outings so that they could be alone in the living room with the beloved. Light poured in upon them like Vermeer's annunciations. If the term for Holy Spirit was masculine in Latin and neuter in Greek, it was feminine in the Hebrew language of the household. Little wonder the Chinese character for 'good' was a diagrammatic simplification of a mother and child, or that Pier Paolo Pasolini would cast his mum as the BVM in his *Gospel According to Saint Matthew*.

Some of the Maries who shaped my childhood had wonderful names, better even than the primal Mariam of the scriptures. Mrs Heritage cleaned the church. Mother Power taught me to read. The Puffin paperbacks on my bookshelves had been mostly written by female authors, just as the gutsy Protestant hymns we sang in the school chapel had been fashioned by valiant bluestocking spinsters in evangelical

England. In the wooden wards of a local hospital, where only the tinny transistor sound of the *Gay Byrne Show* fretted at the institutional silence, elderly incurables with names like Ethel and Iris and Ellen struggled sardonically under candlewick bedspreads for a breath of centrally heated air, for a drop of dull water tasting of toothpaste, showing me as a schoolboy how to practise dying. In the long journey from male adolescence to adulthood, from girlie magazines to grim mammographs, from the songs of the humpback whale on old vinyl records at ante-natal classes to the sympathetic haemorrhoids of the labour wards where I watched my kids being born, I have been guided and guarded by women; and though it has become a cultural commonplace for men to sing in Middle C of such things, the month that is in it moves me to do so, for this is the springtime of Our Lady and the genitals of tulips are opening up again.

The biblical basis for such celebration may be that bit frugal. Part of it is probably pagan. Saint Mark dismisses mother-talk altogether. Family life is no family show in his dark gospel. Later, in the first of her two appearances in the book of John, the virgin emerges in the fable of Cana as a somewhat prehensile Jewish mammy egging on her son to be spectacular at the party. But as long as Luke survives to ease the mannishness of Christianity, a rooted and a radical Mary of Nazareth, mother of God, remains an icon, with all the authority of powerlessness, among the sterile and successful idols of her gender.

As she reappears among us suddenly with altered features in the Mary from Mongolia or from Belarus, as Poles or Filipinas, calling themselves by ordinary English names because their own are unpronounceable and clutching their mobile phone the way our great-grandmothers lugged their Singer sewing machines from shore to shore, we do well to remember the dogged and enduring fragility that befits the Marian image. The Yes, Yes, Yes of Molly Bloom has something of its assent and its enthusiasm, but it's always a note of protest from the periphery and therefore an undefended anthem. In the expert transition from the cult of the Virgin Mother to that of the Virgin Queen in Elizabethan England, Mary's fortunes went to ground in one generation. Devotion died here in a decade, between the time I was in short pants and the time I was in long. We have lost the sense of it altogether. Perhaps the sense of loss has itself been lost.

Erasmus of Rotterdam, the sixteenth-century humanist, speaks for Mary and through her as a sort of secretary in her cri de couer to Glaucoplutus, the grey eyed god of the dead. 'Before this,' she is made to say, 'I was acclaimed as Queen of Heaven and Mistress of the World; but nowadays there are hardly any from whom I hear so much as a Hail Mary. In the old days I was beautified with precious stones and change of clothes … but now I go about in a moth-eaten hand-me-down … Yet you shall not throw me out unless you throw my son out too, whom I hold tight in my arms. I won't be taken from him. You can either reject us or receive us – unless it be your aim to have a Church without a Christ.'

Chapter Nineteen
MISSION POSSIBLE

THIRTY YEARS AGO I used to teach modules in English language and literature to Roman Catholic seminarians in All Hallows College in Drumcondra, Dublin, cycling there twice weekly in a gilly's waterproof raincoat and with bicycle clips round my fashionably flared trousers on a policeman's functional Raleigh, all handle bar and mudguard, with the day's Gestetner hand-outs – poems by Carlos Williams and short stories from Isaac Bashevis Singer – in a cardboard accordion file on the big back carrier. The students, a medley of Blessed Sacrament and Holy Ghost and half a dozen other societies and congregations, were as hirsute as myself, counter-cultural, chain-smoking sorts, more Deep Purple than Palestrina choir, more Led Zeppelin than Laudate Dominum, though none of them rivalled my own Haight Ashbury rig-out from detours into the Dandelion Green, or the Fu Manchu moustache that I had darkened with the aid of a sister's toiletry so that its sand-brown strangeness would blend in better with my otherwise auburn hair.

All of this took place, as you can well imagine, shortly before the great Polish Pope of the present ongoing restoration relinquished his see in the embattled, authoritarian archdiocese of Krakow and began, it seemed to some of us, diligently to double-glaze the dormer windows of the Vatican against a draft of wind that was proving rather too Pentecostal for the temporal powers of the Church. John Paul II, a cornerstone of twentieth-century Christianity, had lived most of his life with the cult of personality in an austere dictatorship that he would ultimately subvert without violence or victimage, and he inevitably transported some elements of the root and branch ecosystem he had known into the GHQ where his new portfolio took him.

A cleric who had inhaled the odour of roast human torso on the wind during the second world war could not be expected to hum 'Here Comes the Sun' at any stage in his pontificate; and yet the recollection of the expression of episcopal disgust on his face at his robustly rapturous reception in the chapel in Maynooth College in 1979 always reminds me sadly and simultaneously of those lost, lovable All Hallows alumni with their mandolins, their grammars of the Yoruba and Hausa languages, the barricade bravery of their thirst for social justice, and the enormous, silent aquarium of tropical fish at another house of studies in the capital where it was not at all unknown for one particular candidate for the priesthood to insert himself at night in swimming togs or in no togs at all, just to float there in the submarine beatitude of mere being, among the timid, technicolor schools of orchid dottybacks and kissing gourami, copperband butterfly fish and the stolid, self-effacing chocolate chip starfish that lay like the Star of David, the deputy badge of the bogey man, embedded in grit and gravel at the bottom of the tank.

This isn't meant to be a funereal theme, a fadó, fadó, let alone an ochón, ochón ó. Marvellous things have happened in the meantime, not the least of which is All Hallows' own radical rejuvenation as a contemporary mission institute, with an outflow of apostolic women preaching and practising in the pagan savannah of the Irish dormitory suburbs and the polytheistic, idol infested interior of the Dublin urban bourgeoisie. For the heart of darkness, as Conrad recognised a hundred years ago, is closer to us than the forest gloom of the Congo. It beats its terrible tom-tom in the gong that summons us daily into our mahogany dining rooms. In any event, the revolutionary threshold of every era almost invariably turns out to be a revolving door, and the gospel – or the *aggelia*, the 'message', as Saint John prefers to call it – was probably betrayed from the moment that, after due scribal deliberation on his part, the author of Saint Matthew replaced Saint Luke's 'Blessed are the poor' with his more genteel and gradualistic 'Blessed are the poor in spirit', since the Kingdom, all things considered, would probably require a permanent salaried bureaucracy close to the throne.

But there was still something splendid in the chiselled lintel of the college in Drumcondra with its Latin imperative in those crisp, capital letters – *Euntes, docete omnes gentes*: Go therefore and teach all nations! – which, while it doesn't come from the mouth and mindset of the historical Jesus whose concern was always for the House of Jacob and not for the Gentile world, does incarnate superbly the breakthrough Christian vision of his earliest followers in a mission statement and a missiology that have only faltered in our own lifetime with the loss of faith in all things European and the mortal, self-harming masochism of its client intelligentsia.

Today we don't know what to teach or to whom, what to proclaim, what to protest, what to protest against. We speak of enculturation instead of evangelisation. We speak of an African Christ instead of a Christian Africa. We speak in the deferential vernacular of faith and culture instead of the abusive bully pulpit of the past. We are right, of course to be diagonal and diplomatic. Pianissimo too can be a forte. But in the five-hundredth anniversary year of the birth of Francis Xavier, it can appear at times that we have lost our note, if not our nerve. The white-headed boys who set out for the two-thirds world in my childhood are white-haired geriatrics now, watching fortune tellers on breakfast television from their commode wheelchairs in retirement homes around the country, in a culture which cares nothing whatsoever for the stories of their sorties to the South world or for the history of their dizzy zeal among the persecuted likenesses of God. Yet the friends I made immediately in America when I worked there twenty-five years ago were undergraduates of every race and religion from shanty towns and Bantustans worldwide who had been taught by Christian Brothers, trained by Spiritans and Mercy sisters, vaccinated by the Medical Missionaries, radicalised by Jesuits, unionised by Dominicans, and whose Zambian or Filipino English brimmed with the Irish idioms of Donegal and Limerick.

Such street cred or cachet as I possessed among these scholarship sorts proceeded from their esteem and affection for a church catholic that had differed routinely and resolutely from the norms of force in their native countries and, by so differing, had made all the difference. To most of us who stayed home and got Mass, mention of blasphemy would bring to mind attention-seeking artefacts like the Piss Christ, a crucifix suspended in a pint of the artist's urine, or the diapered Pierrot playing Jesus in *The Jerry Springer Show*, but to the footloose missionaries with their ludicrous optimism, the supreme blasphemy was the poverty and oppression of the speechless majority who are pregnant with hunger below a certain line on any atlas.

Here in Ireland it's almost summer. Mothers will be doing Lough Derg soon in the hope that their daughters get the points for Medicine, or ringing their mobiles from the landline to find out where they left them last. The dads will be sipping fair trade coffee in their Spanish holiday homes, where the bodies of smuggled North African immigrants wash up each morning among the banana boats on the private beaches. For, in spite of the years of Mary Robinson, the place we're in is looking less and less like Mary of Nazareth and more and more like Robinson Crusoe, less a matter of dogged discipleship for the sake of community than the entrepreneurial economics of hunter-gathering for the four walls of one's own fort. Those of us who cannot be saved by the art of business strive instead to be redeemed by the business of art. At the sight of a revolver we reach fastidiously for our culture. But can lithographs and the Penguin library protect us from the rising waters of the deep when the Father of Jesus comes to drown out the doting Father Christmas we have dared to put in his place?

Perhaps it has taken the presence of Muslim refugees in Jonathan Swift's witnessing cathedral to remind us all that a sanctuary is not simply for the birds, and that a church exists for more than the Veni, Vidi, Victimhood of our little, privatised afflictions. It exists to summon the rejoicing neighbour out of James Joyce's nigh boor; it exists to summon a people out of predatory rivals, just as the Irish word 'muintir' still glints italically with the silverfish of its origin in the Latin for 'monastery'. It exists, in fact, to enter with open arms into the sin and zen of the real world. It is not about the blue beyond in the hereafter, but about going beyond the beyond in the here and now, in the risk and jeopardy of outreach.

Today's first reading from the Book of Acts reports the epochal meeting between the Galilean Simon Peter and the God-fearing centurion Cornelius. That encounter smashed from the very start the sectarian strictures and suspicions on both sides, transforming a separatist party of messianic Jews into an assimilationist community with a universal agenda and a professional military presence into a cooperative partner. The tactical pro-Roman elements in the narratives of the New Testament, modified as they were to enable ease of passage for the breakaway faith through the vigilant empire, cannot prevent the utter astonishment of the account from bursting through at the very thought of the spectacle it records. This is the meeting in mutuality of the camp inmate and the camp guard, of the occupied and the occupier, the oppressor and the oppressed. The King James Version gives verse 26 as 'Peter took him up, saying, "Stand up. I myself also am a man"'; and the Jerusalem translation offers 'Peter helped him up. "Stand up," he said. "I am only a man after all."' But the two verbs in the verse are explicit Resurrection terms, and synonyms for the sake of elegant variation obscure the point. The line could be read instead as saying, 'Peter raised him up, saying, "Be risen; be resurrected. I too am a human being just as you are."'

It is that Easter exuberance we need again now, the radiant recognition that the deep humanity of God tends and intends us all. The supposedly jingoistic missiology of my youth may have been superseded by a respectful and a relativistic defeatism in face of sheer cultural diversity, but the ranks of the broken-hearted baptised increase and multiply. A friend of mine has told me that, in two recent forays to a crematorium, he had been consoled but not convinced by a traditional service, replete with the Rosary, and convinced but not consoled by a multi-faith, postmodern one, complete with poetry from the Norton anthology. So the new mission frontier is often internal, an in-between place. Hairline fractures inhabit us all. Cracks in the crystal soul make it hard to tell commitment from cultural nostalgia, ministry from the administration of habit. Those outside or sent there in reprisal, the graced, the God-fearing, the excluded sweethearts of the Holy Spirit, are growing in need and number all the while. It is Peter's moment. It is this Easter exuberance we need now, where only the deep humanity of God can truly divine us. The jingoistic missiology of my youth may have miscarried, to be sure, but mission opportunities abound locally.

The very Vatican, whose name in Latin denotes a place of prophecy, has so confused ministry with administration, that it's left largely to the Anglican Communion in our time to be the Petri dish of the perennial experiment that we call the Christian way. For the counter-intuitive recreation of human nature, which is the great semitic gift to our species, occurs not only as an oratory but as a laboratory as well.

Chapter Twenty
THE LATIN FOR 'IGNORAMUS'

WASN'T IT THE EIGHTEENTH-CENTURY Anglican priest Sydney Smith who remarked that he never read a book he'd been asked to review in case it prejudiced his opinion of it? Like that loveable and enlightened figure, I haven't seen *The Da Vinci Code*, partly because I dislike the importunity of intercontinental publicists and partly because its premises and plotline are as ludicrous, though not as shameful or as sinister, as the *Protocols of the Elders of Zion*; but the movie has energised the more dogged bloggers on some of my favourite Internet websites, and it's also served to exhibit precipitous degrees of ignorance about fundamentals of faith among ordinary cultural Christians.

Not that I don't savour work from the wayside, shoreline stuff that challenges kitsch and counterfeit piety of every kind. The controversial Madonna made from elephant dung, for instance, seemed to me an incarnational image, tough, tender and theologically truthful. Monty Python's *Life of Brian*, drawing as it does on the benevolent ironies of the best traditions of Christian humanism, has sustained me in the small hours of unhappiness, and, in its deconstruction of sectarianism and shrill spirituality, is altogether a more fortunate film than Mel Gibson's fatal attempt at atonement. But the ability to read and relish the heterodox resides in a thoroughgoing knowledge of orthodoxy itself. We can't be enriched by variations on a theme unless and until we know the theme by heart. Margins and mainstream reveal themselves only in their relationship. At the very least, we live in a world of compare and contrast, where mind is a function of memory, where initial leave to learn is the prerequisite of eventual learning to leave, where we do not inhabit the moment merely, as those appalling tranquillity tapes will tell us, but where instead we range at all times across the conflict and the clarity of the whole table of tenses. Just as the modern retina can no longer construe indiscriminate greenery in the way pre-historic humans had to in order to forage and feed themselves, so the deterioration of our religious and cultural traditions in the contemporary world results in a grey glaucoma, a lack of peripheral vision that makes the landscape featureless, unfocussed.

Recently I overheard a middle-aged woman in a canteen deploring the practice of churching which she had been reading about indignantly in a Sunday supplement at the solarium. Her rage and resentment on behalf of her gender was directed audibly at the supposed phallic, priest-ridden, patriarchal institution that has always pissed on half the population from a height. In fact, her anger was such that I thought the better of informing her that the ceremony of churching, an English translation of which may be found in the *Book of Common Prayer*, registers heartfelt and tearful thanksgiving to God that mum has survived the mortal peril of childbirth in a world which, until my father's time, in the late thirties of the last century, relied on the most rudimentary interventions to ease distress or avert complication. Had she been foul-mouthing rabbis or imams in the same style, she might have been prosecuted under the Incitement to Hatred Act. As it was, she was only taking her turn at the shrieking karaoke microphone.

Ignorance, the open university of *sancta simplicitas*, is in part the product of the collapse of catechesis and courses in Church history during the 70s, when, as I recall vividly, civics and an anecdotal semblance of sex education ousted the kind of scripture study, actual Talmudic instruction, without which religion, the incarnational community, declines inevitably into solipsistic candlelight and the crooning of Kahlil Gibran. Even the continuing newspaper correspondence about the inter-Church concelebration of a Mass in Drogheda by a low Augustinian and a high Anglican priest suggests, among those contributors who congratulate the rite, an ahistorical and impoverished sense of the richly diverse traditions and theologies of the sacrament. By despising such festive distinctiveness in the name of a grand gesture, this desire for the unitary rather than the unified obliterates the merits of our multitudinous embodiments of the gift of God's Eucharist. It encourages anti-intellectualism, and reifies the action of bread-breaking, obsessing, with a sort of mass hysteria, over emblematic church ceremony instead of stressing the real presence of the crucified and risen One in every inclusive act of hospitality, the world over, as well as in solemn liturgical remembrance.

Poet Dennis O'Driscoll provides definitive testimony to the slow subsidence of the religious realm in Ireland in his wry and wistful canticle 'Missing God', in which he plays in G minor upon idioms of nostalgia for a referential world that is sinking into extinction like the bird of paradise and the humble honey bee. And it was with the very same writer, my dear, dissimilar twin, that I visited the Museo de Bellas Artes in the city of Seville ten years ago now. There, in what had been for centuries a Cistercian precinct of the strict observance, hung an abundance of art works by the likes of the Cretan painter El Greco and the local boy, Francisco de Zurbaran, canvases little and large that all originated in the mother tongue of Judeo-Christianity, the vernacular of Europe for two astounding, wounded millennia. Every myth, metaphor and motif of that language was on show: scriptural scenarios, sacramental signs, the whole transformational grammar of the ground of our sinful civilisation.

Yet the rented audiocassettes that directed the two of us in standard English through our individual silicone headphones from one easel painting to another assumed complete incomprehension amongst the high-culture, category AB consumers who were moving from precious object to precious object like the elderly folk of my infancy doing the stations of the cross in Donnybrook Church on their way to the butcher's or the post office. In the cushioned ear-piece, cultural interpreters, the new priesthood of postmodernity, elucidated even the scenes of the Nativity and the Crucifixion for the browsing bourgeois sorts whose Blue Guide is the Bible of the gap year and the walkabout sabbatical from one cashpoint to another.

Truly it could be thought that the devotees have replaced the devout, and oils and acrylic efface the holy oils as the currency of the cultivated man. The bread and wine of Mass culture has become bread and circuses for the proles, wine and cheese for the occupying class, and bread and water for the photogenic populations of poor countries. We seek now in aesthetic gratification the tremulous epiphanies that are only really available in the mythical magi's quest, in the down-and-dirty comradeship of sufferance and suffering, in Yeats' 'shed of experience'. Worse, the aesthetic moment has matured into the anaesthetic eternity of personal introversion, so that even atrocity, be it the World Trade Centre or the Asian tsunami, can pleasure the sensibility as a cathartic form of televisual beauty on the plasma screens that have eclipsed the wall hangings of an earlier era.

So the cultured humanitarian triumphs over the Christian witness to the point where it's possible to reverse, by the strategic adjustment of its very last noun from its original 'temples', the infamous boast of Tertullian to the startled pagan sophisticates of Rome: 'We're recent arrivals, but we've already spread everywhere – from capital cities to outlying islands, centres of power, areas of high-density population, debating chambers, local government, parliament, the press, supermarkets and shopping centres. We have left you nothing at all except the churches you worship in.'

The single most serious consequence of all this isn't, of course, the poignant word-of-mouth which tells you that an Irish film director had to coach his millennial adolescent extras both in blessing themselves and in genuflecting for the chapel scenes in his period screenplay, or in the short-sighted delight that a fifty-something documentary maker appeared to evince when a present-day pupil at his former Christian Brothers' school was perplexed by a simple question from the pre-conciliar penny catechism. It isn't either the gobbledygook, more balder than dash, that's being spoken at the moment about Jesus of Nazareth and Mary Magdalene, the historic apostle to the apostles, although that ancient gossip deeply misrepresents the Lord's singularity by stressing his state as a singleton. The community of those who believe preserve in the present and for posterity the memory of Jesus' solitariness not as a flight from the flesh – the Incarnation is the very opposite of that – but as a heroic witness to powerlessness as the green venue of the proper authority of God, a choice that theologian Sean Freyne explores in his beautiful, book-length meditation entitled *Jesus, a Jewish Galilean*. As someone who had made himself a eunuch for the sake of the kingdom by forgoing the patriarchal privileges of chattel and child, which were the defining attributes of masculinity in the male order of Palestinian Judaism, Jesus exemplified the very marginality that he ministered to in his unprecedented openness to others, many of them vulnerable women on the deserted outskirts of the territory he crossed, to all of whom he brought, in James Alison's felicitous phrase, the good news that God not only loved them but liked them as well.

Perhaps because I was raised by Jesuits who would clean the chalk dust from the teacher's table with the black wing of their soutane and settle down to reminisce from the sunlit wooden rostrum in the prep-school classroom about their fraternal forebears, the Counter-Reformation astronomers, botanists, chemists, cosmologists, economists, geographers, geologists, linguists, all the early Ignatian pathfinders and polymaths from Matteo Ricci to Athanasius Kirchner, I am baffled most of all these days by the unexamined ease with which those pillars of society, the newspaper columnists, assume and affirm an antagonism between Christianity and the Enlightenment. So far from being obtuse and obscurantist, a troglodyte struggling with the angel of scientific rationality, the Church gave birth to the Enlightenment, just as the cloister created the quad, and the monastery brought the university into being. The entire history of the project we call the European heritage, both in its oratories and in its laboratories, chapels and council chambers, parliaments and presses, in its stealthy, inchmeal evolution of personal rights and public responsibility, stems from the biblical anthropology which privileges victims. Against the incremental vengeance which is the conventional basis of the social order as a balanced, retaliatory infrastructure, the idea of Europe emerged almost imperceptibly, particle by particle, as a fragile, fearful disposition to begin imagining the Beatitudes.

For, if Athens gave us the citizen, Jerusalem gave us the human person; if Greece gave us the collectivity, Israel gave us the community. The Greek term for an individual, cited most famously in Pericles' oration on democracy during the Peloponnesian war, is the word 'idiot"; but the individual human being derives his or her ultimate dignity from the texts and contexts of the Passion narratives in which an excluded other becomes the norm of selfhood, and from the Eucharistic services which tirelessly exalt the casualties of our own violence.

Chapter Twenty-One
A DIFFERENT DRUMBEAT

THE GREAT NOBEL PRIZE-WINNING German novelist Günter Grass published *The Tin Drum*, the first volume of his celebrated Danzig trilogy, around the time I was born in the mid-fifties of the last century; and for my generation in Ireland, as for his own in the Federal Republic where he combined the solitary life of an author with the civic life of a left-of-centre intellectual in Willy Brandt's Social Democratic Party, his writings and his witness embodied a wise and passionate humanism in a culture which had worshipped strange and savage gods. These were the post-war decades in which, against massive institutional reticence in reconstructed West Germany, prophetic persons like Grass and Heinrich Boll and Gert Hofman were in difficult dialogue with the Nazi period. Aryan Germany had continued to supply much of the judicial, academic and business infrastructure for Chancellor Adenauer's economic miracle; for, in the bipolar world of the new superpower stand-off between the USA and the USSR, the Americanised Prussian eagle had risen as a phoenix from a fatherland in ashes, and the task of 'Vergangenheitsbewältigung', of coming to terms with the past, was stoutly resisted.

Without the self-incriminating testimony of the new fiction writers who had submitted themselves as enthusiastic conscripts in the millenarian crusades of the Third Reich, that past would not have become sufficiently present to make any future possible. They operated as fabulists among confabulators, storytellers among tell-tales; and their discourse freed, or at any rate, freed up, the generation of the 1960s. I spent the heady summer of 1968 with a German family whose father had soldiered with the Wehrmacht in the Soviet Union, and I remember his hardback bedside copy of *Mein Kampf* with the agitated pencil annotations in which he struggled to understand the hypnotic tantrum of the drumming he had marched to, back in the teenage years when he should have been dreaming of women's underwear and not of men's uniforms. His transformation – his 'turning' to use the more straightforward biblical verb of conversion – had probably been prompted in part by Gunter Grass's dense, disarming parables, among them the silencing din of *The Tin Drum* whose staccato startled Europe in a speak easy, say nothing season.

Now Grass has himself been drummed out of the regiment of the righteous. In an early August 2006 newspaper interview with *Frankfurter Allgemeine Zeitung*, the idolised octogenarian admitted for the first time to having served in a Waffen SS Panzer division as a seventeen-year-old during the firestorm finale of the second world war. His silence on the subject over a long lifetime is, in its turn, considered unspeakable by his accusers who are themselves anything but speechless. The conservative daily *Die Welt* has announced that 'the end of his tenure as a moral authority is now here'; Cologne's *Stadt-Anzeiger* asserted that 'his droning silence sounds a bit pathological and a little bit cowardly'; *Suddeutsche Zeitung* stated that the writer had undermined his credibility, and the left-wing *Die Tageszeitung* wondered aloud if his discretion hadn't been a stratagem to avert the forfeiture of the inevitable Nobel booty. The Central Council of Jews in Germany believes, according to the *Spiegel* online English Site, that this act of withholding invalidates earlier witness, and Grass's biographer Michael Jurgs, quoted in the *London Times*, delivers himself of the opinion that his subject's confessional lapse 'puts in doubt from a moral point of view anything he has ever told us'.

Denunciation is, of course, our daily bread. Goethe said that the Irish will always pull down the white stag, but his own compatriots were and remain no different. It is the nature of nature, which is after all the precarious cultural enterprise of a singular species that is always absorbed in the work of the one and the many, of sorting and sorting out. Ask a man what he most despises and he will tell you what he most desires. Inversely, infatuation is to resentment what the egg is to the imago, the unlikely and essential antecedent. Sooner or later, our valentines will turn into vitriol as the stage we have built for our heroes becomes their scaffold. In standing before us, they have dared to stand beyond us; and, in standing beyond us, they stand against us. The encounter has become a confrontation. Moreover, it was they who started it, not us. Once they were ravishing mentors. Now they are tormentors who have raped us. They were bogus from the beginning. We had always suspected it. Only our great good nature stopped us from saying so. But the Law must take its course at last.

Why Grass grassed on himself, as it were, is another matter. Perhaps he could not bear the scapegoat solitude of his own purity as an idol and an icon, an intolerable, sterile template for his furious, infuriated admirers. 'Perfection is terrible, it cannot have children', Sylvia Plath remarks pregnantly in one of her poems, and perhaps Grass could no longer endure his own posterity as a public statue and a pigeon roost. The thought might have petrified him, a full-grown man whose proper majesty is to be flesh and blood in the mere chemistry of the universe; because it is we humans and we humans alone whose community as a mess of mucous membrane, as fallen and therefore as fertile individuals on a small and insignificant planet, transfigures the antibiotic laboratory of the cosmos into a dirty oratory where we go on all fours towards our blinding biographies. Imperfection is, in fact, our forte, and moral maturity arises, if at all, only from strenuous, conflicted lives, and not from the clinical increments of academic decency. If our struggle with spirituality does not leave us limping like the poor patriarch in the Book of Genesis, we cannot inherit or bequeath to our own seed and breed the new name Israel, a Hebrew expression that signifies 'wrestling with God', which Jacob bestowed upon his house in the middle Bronze Age.

The move from the truth of myth to the data of history reports the same finding. In the topographical language of Exodus, the path to the Promised Land lies through the Wilderness of Sin. The classical counterparts are the Homeric poems and they endorse this itinerary across the Aegean archipelago: there can be no Odyssey without an Iliad. To overcome ourselves we must first undergo ourselves, and that same undertaking, as the very verb implies, consists in a twofold exercise of spadework: first the drastic excavation of our past motives and then the dreadful burial of our present being. Whether in the figures of digging or drowning, of submersion in floodwater or entombment in the ground, of sea change or seed time, this process was once called 'baptism'. It has long since sunk and ebbed away into a photogenic, lukewarm dribble in a pre-booked baptistery where we daub or dunk our babies. It has softened into a centrally heated rite of registration and club membership that entitles one to a wedding and/or funeral in the same space later; but in its turbulent birth on the banks of the Jordan River when camelhair-coated, cult leader John administered the rite to a naked Galilean pilgrim called Yeshua ben Yosef of Nazareth, baptism described an act of personal disintegration and death as the necessary prior condition of full and fulfilling life. It enacted an inundation, the deluge out of which dry land at last arises. As Martin Buber observes, 'the idea of allowing oneself to sink and take root in the ground that men call despair, the ground in which self-destruction and rebirth occur – that would be the start of turning.'

The famished forms of contemporary christenings know nothing of dying and rising. Our own wistful Christianity has largely forgotten it. But the new Irish are getting along swimmingly. On the Dart from Dún Laoghaire into centre-city Dublin, I saw from the Seapoint embankment a baptismal cluster of West Africans in white, light linen, wind-blown gowns walking down slowly into the snot-green, salt water where I used to wring my togs and rinse my snorkel in the goose-pimpled good old days when everybody had an uncle or an aunt on the foreign missions, and the Biafran national anthem was sung to the air of 'A Nation Once Again'. The recently arrived, whether refugee or migrant, recall more accurately than the indigenous rest of us the Christ whose empty tomb establishes him forever as the prototype of the disappeared of history and whose continuing cult exists to place the unlisted and the blacklisted casualty at the centre of our culture.

To do this we must first reveal our own violence. We must die a death and be reconceived. A psychotherapy which reconfigures victimisers as victims falls short of our searching. The innocence of the neo-natal child, neatly enveloped in the family heirloom of a christening shawl, cannot help us either, for the crisis of conversion is a wholly adult affair. It is all risk and jeopardy, a going down and a going under. It is a rendezvous with the *tohu wa bohu*, the formless void and darkness upon the face of the deep. The narrative of the baptism of Jesus in the earliest gospel understands this well. While the later iconography of the Church and the lectionary selections in the liturgy emphasise God's congratulatory address from the blue beyond and the sudden, stunning plummet of the dove, Mark insists that 'immediately the Spirit driveth him into the wilderness; and he was there in the wilderness forty days, tempted of Satan; and was with the wild beasts; and the angels ministered to him'.

We are ordained by our troubles and our tragedies, not by college diplomas. The patron saints of my community are Peter and Paul, not just because their dialectic of tradition and modernity drives the Church forward into the future, but because their ultimate apostolic authority is grounded in the proteins of personal failure. Peter can achieve fidelity only because he has first committed betrayal; Paul can champion non-violence only because he has brothers' blood on his hands. It is hard contradiction that grows us and graduates us, not facile consistency. The early life of any saint worth his salt, from Augustine to Ignatius, bears this out. So the Polish Archbishop Joseph Michalik was right to recommend Gunter Grass's candour. 'I think,' said the prelate, 'he is a greater man today for having confessed while excusing others. I think he is a greater authority and a greater writer than he was before.' The same elderly embattled eminence, one of whose essays in the late twentieth century sponsored the forty shades of grey as a more suitable spectrum than the forty shades of green, should know in his heart of hearts that this is indeed the gospel truth.

Chapter Twenty-Two
A PICTURE IN THE ATTIC

A LARGE PICTURE OF JESUS hung over the mantlepiece in my parents' bedroom forty years ago. It may have been a copy of a Murillo, the seventeenth-century Iberian artist so identified with mass-culture Catholicism and commodity religious images that, in his native country, his name still signifies discount devotionalism today. Handsome to the point of being hermaphroditic, the long-haired Lord that looked out of his three-quarter length portrait at the candlewick bedspread and the complementary candlewick side-lights on their two bedside tables was at least slender, sallow and semitic. In fact, he bore an unnerving resemblance to Osama bin Laden, with one punctured hand bestowing a blessing on the two dachshunds, Cindy and Maximilian, who snored in front of the gas fire and the other pointing like a post-mortem at the technicolor Catherine wheel of his heart. The previous fashion in the face of Christ, which I could examine in my grandparent's apartments up and down the road, favoured a more blonde and body-built Scandinavian saviour, closer to Valhalla than to Galilee, a Nordic predilection that had probably stemmed from the nineteenth-century biblical scholarship, much of it German, alas, which had often disputed and sometimes altogether denied Jesus' embarrassing Jewishness.

The painting didn't last, of course. By the early 1970s the Irish bourgeoisie had evacuated lots of its ancestral cultural abracadabra lest cosmopolitan visitors snigger at the sight of it. Less kitsch, more cutting edge, a study of Jesus, done as an aide mémoire for a stained glass commission by the former Anglican nun Evie Hone, ousted the melancholy Old Master, and poor Murillo ended up beside the water tank in under the eaves, among life jackets and fishing rods and a pail of pink rat killer, like a Jew hiding in terror from the gentile militia. He had become again what he had started out as, an undocumented individual, a refugee on the run, a menaced, marginal presence; or, as the newest Oxford English Dictionary defines it: 'Jesus – a strong exclamation of surprise, disbelief or dismay, as in *by Jesus, Jesus H. Christ, and Jesus wept*,' the last expression of which from John's gospel is, by the way, the shortest verse in scripture apart from 'Rejoice exceedingly!'

I suppose I'd like to think that the portrait is still there, wedged damply beneath the roof slates in the thin bronchitis of their winter whining, but the probable truth is that the darkness of that A-frame garret is a blinding en suite now, with Habitat mirrors repeating our nakedness to infinity like a transcendental number, the decimal forms of Pi. Anyhow, it remains the picture in the attic over most of the country as the old babyish mythology of the star-child continues to yield ground, year by year, to the new Babylonian mythology of scientific rationality, and we go on absailing into the abyss of our own bottomlessness with ropes made from the newest synthetic filaments.

If I think tonight of the Murillo in my parent's bedroom, it's partly because I could never understand how my dad, who was more of a Moravian than a Bohemian, would pray to and through such a feminine image of maleness while despising my pony-tail as a social delinquency amounting to a sexual deviancy (he would make me stuff it down the neck of my shirt at his sailing club). I think of it as well because of the memory of my mother and my father with their dressing gowns on, undressing away from each other, with their backs turned. Was this a proof of the dreariness of their intercourse in the vilified 1950s or a plenary mark of its accomplished eroticism in the time before obstetrical pornography made vaginas a yawn? We cannot look at the act of lovemaking which began our own being in the world anymore than we can look at a solar eclipse without ruining our retinas. It is as personal and as prohibited as the climax of our dying. For the beginning and the end of our individuality have been hidden from us in ultraviolet and in infrared lest we should entertain ideas above our station. Yet I, along with all my siblings, had been conceived, an infinitesimal blastocyst in need of nothing but the warm endurance of duration, under that same brooding, bisexual gaze on the chimneypiece; and its dim medium, its mild, unsmiling finality, would accompany me throughout my childhood, sometimes as encounter, sometimes as confrontation, in alternating cycles of complicity and conflict. After all, I had been raised so unselfconsciously in the Latinized language of the missals that I mistook the adverb in the earliest words I ever learned to sing:

> Row, row, row the boat
> Gently down the stream.
> Verily, verily, verily, verily,
> Life is but a dream.

As I struggled towards puberty, as the first corkscrew hairs question-marked my pubis, as the sated bluebottles of an African atrocity seethed behind the television screen in our living room, and as the charismatic priests of my prep-school years pined for teargas and a tour of duty in Central America, the face persisted.

It could still be Sephardic, olive-skinned and oriental, but its oddball mobility had started to suggest itself in stranger profiles than the set-piece Bedouin swami of the new acrylic icons in the inner-city bedsits where Belfield undergraduates lit joss sticks and listened to each other's stomach noises after a cramped snog on a beanbag. It wasn't only, as the satirical Soviet magazine *Krokodil* remarked, that every male who could shave looked like the Saviour. The tears of Christ watermarked more than the fuchsia bushes. Even the silver of your own weeping on the sleeves of your pullover could be precious metal. You could see him in the rioting tyros at the barricades. You could see him in the frightened, flint-like faces behind the visors of police helmets. You could see him in the human heronries at the gates of death camps. Indeed, as our species strained the elasticity of the lithosphere to breaking point, you could even distinguish his primitive facies in pencil in the monastic patience of our outlawed in-law, the orang-utan. Just as your saffron monk in a Sri Lankan temple can recapitulate the Buddha's steep, impenetrable smile, so the photo-fit full face of Jesus the Jew, the age-old graffito of the excluded soloist and not the handy totem of a dominant state, migrates, whenever we allow ourselves to let it, from all its crippling, cultic stereotypes to inhabit, time and again, the definitively human as the norm of the natural. The Lord of hosts is not primarily the major-domo of the ciborium, but our authentic likeness. No-one has the least idea what he looked like; everybody can identify him. So far from being the Olympian enigma of our desperate anthropomorphosis, he is the one completely human presence in a polytheistic world.

Today's gospel (Mark 8:27-33) in the catholic Christian roster of readings repeats a lection that was used some months ago in the season of length, the lengthening of the light – or, as the Anglo-Saxons used to call it, the season of Lent. The same Socratic story, the same Q and A, occurs in each of the three synoptic texts, as Jesus asks in the Greek approximation of his original Aramaic utterance: *Humeis de tina me legete einai?* Who do you say that I am? We know already from the previous verses that his greatest admirers compare and contrast him routinely to some titanic Israelite predecessors, both to Elijah the prophet and even to the leader of the Exodus, the primordial path finder with the Egyptian name of Moses, a semi-historical figure who met the Almighty face-to-face or, as the Hebrew expression actually indicates, 'mouth to mouth'. In fact, the Christian tale of the transfiguration, a theological legend that immediately follows each account of Jesus' question to his disciples, deliberately plagiarises for purely pictorial purposes many literary motifs in the story of the superpower summit on the top of Mount Sinai in order to enact the moment of Peter's decision as a screenplay, to change it from catechesis to costume drama, to make it fully present, just as Saint Mark himself delights to swerve into the present out of the past tense – for his literal language reads 'and he says to them, "Who do you say I am", and Peter … says to him, "you are the anointed".' You are the Christ.

If I'd been asked the question at any time during my adolescence or early adulthood, I would have replied with talk of three persons and two natures. Such discourse, be it said, would not have been intelligible either to the historical Jesus or to his little entourage after his death; and much of the modern world will find it as arcane as any Pythagorean theorem. This is not an attempt on my part, as my father once grandly alleged, to reduce the mystical body to the lowest common denomination. Instead, it's a desire to trace a series to the wellspring of its source in gushing water. The enigma of Jesus first generated the mystery of the Christ. Talk of the Christ inaugurated Christology. In turn, Christology constructed Trinitarian thinking, an intellectual marvel that would itself be deflected eventually into the messianic Marxist dialectic. But it begins under the olives. It begins in the high hysteria of the insects during the concussion of noon. It begins with a circle of men delousing each other on the road to Jerusalem. It begins in the Mediterranean, which is to say quite literally that it starts in the very middle of this world. I am trying to disengage the magician from the man so that his humanity, which is the template of the truth of our nature, can begin to divine me. I am trying to set aside the haggling, agile verbiage of my prayer life, which, like most tranquillity tapes and our daily manoeuvres on prayer mats, is really a strategy of negotiation, a protocol of control, in order to discover in the octave of its aftermath the priority of the Word where it does not lie: in the unspeaking, in the speechless, and in the unspeakable. We think at times that the life of Jesus is a mere mood swing in our Maker's disposition, a tin whistle amongst the kettledrums, a minor chord of miserable vulnerability in an otherwise majestic movement. But in fact the life of Jesus is the death of God as we knew him.

Chapter Twenty-Three
CREATIONS

A WEEK AFTER my brother John died in the late 1970s, I was having dinner with my parents and a visiting priest friend, when my mother broke down in tears over the main course, which was coq au vin, a family staple. Now I had seen her grieve before but always with decorum and great good manners. This time, however, there was no shot at sangfroid. Secretions came out of her nose as well as her eyes as she wailed like a woman from the Third World. It reminded me, in fact, of the verb Saint John uses in his thumbnail sketch of Jesus lamenting at the hole in the wall where the body of Lazarus is beginning to stink; because, if I'm right in remembering, 'brimazein', the Johannine term applied to the Lord's breakdown and/or breakthrough at the stench of his friend's cadaver, means to snort and salivate like a horse.

Such was my mother's state that night. Her make-up darkened her eyes to the blue-black pastels of domestic bruises. You would think someone had beaten her up, as she stared at the dead breast on her dinner plate and said to it in a wet, child-like way quite unlike her denotative daily tone: 'When I meet him in Heaven, will I recognise him as my son and will he recognise me as his mother? That's all I want to know." I said nothing, because I needed to be aware of everything that was happening at that moment so that I could report it to the far future as a difficult and fitting gift from an obliterated past. And the priest beside me said nothing too, either because he was much too young at thirty-something to have had the experience of loving and losing, which is the Indo-European root work of our pain at all passing, or because he didn't believe in the Resurrection as accurate reportage but as symbolic narrative, which is an occupational hazard of religious life. Instead he bowed his head and found the pattern on his plate, men with hats on standing in a river, a sudden revelation.

But my dad waded right in. He delivered himself of a faltering tutorial about the history of the Judeo-Christian belief in what my dead brother, having been a lawyer when he was well enough to work, liked to call the hereinafter: how there was no mention of the next world in the Hebrew Bible, how the topic was controverted by the rivalrous Pharisees (who believed) and Sadducees (who didn't) during the inter-testamental period, and how credence eventually gained ground to the point of general concurrence in both rabbinic Judaism and primitive Christianity. My mother hiccupped her way through this painstaking pep talk. I suppose she understood that my father's habit was to detoxify any rogue emotion by placing it in an analytic quarantine. That was his form of forty days in the desert; and something of the parental gene must be present in my own physiology since I was rather relieved when we quit the table for the TV and watched *Doctor Zhivago*. There's nothing like a good old weepie to make you feel better.

My reason for reminiscing hasn't, however, to do with resurrection or Resurrectionists (if I may thieve that title from the enterprising body snatchers of Victorian vaudeville) but with contemporary Creationists and with their declared literalism when it comes to the reading of sacred scripture. The current guesstimate is that fully one quarter of American evangelicals anticipate Armageddon with some gusto, and are quite persuaded that the apocalyptic arrow of time has the Middle East in its sights as the ultimate bullseye of its target board. In that sense, their eschatology and my mum's awkward expectations of eternity converge in a shared preoccupation with Last Things. But the equal solicitude of the fundamentalists for first things, for the gorgeous Priestly narrative in the Pentateuch as it unfolds its stately seven-day wonder of a world in the first chapter of the Book of Genesis, is less terrifying. Indeed, it is the very opposite: it is terrified – and terrified, I think, for the same reason that my poor mum, at the other end of the Bible, astray in the curious Resurrection stories of the early Jewish Christians, went a bit demented in her later years until she disappeared out of sight in a psychosis of sorrow which the men in her life, whether physicians or metaphysicians, could not ameliorate. In both cases, the fundamentalists on the one side and my family circumstance on the other, the candour of the old relationship between readers and writings had been fatally compromised by modernity.

Once there was lectio divina, the contemplation of the incandescent Word of God in the chapter and verse of the Hebrew Bible and its Christian codicil. For both religions, parent and child, this practice yielded ample emblematic meanings over millennia, layer upon layer, level after level, a plenitude of possible depths in every detail. But the evidential base of all such exegesis was assumed. Now there's not only the explication of texts but the explication of their pretexts and their subtexts and their contexts, the erudite secular scrutiny of a cultural and conditioned deposit of writings; and, as the historical-critical tradition of biblical interpretation begins to acquire both a pedigree and a patina, traditionalists are dismayed by the instability of the metaphors and the stories in which they had made a most vulnerable act of trust. Holy writ has been mutating into wholesome literature. We can choose to scoff at the supposed Appalachian hillbillies who endorse the puritan Archbishop Ussher's arithmetic, according to which we celebrated the earth's six-thousandth birthday on Saturday 23 October 2004 at 3:00 in the morning; but our denigration is only a failure of the faculty of imagination, for, if we really believed what we know to be true – or, better still, truth-ful – that the universe is at least fourteen billion years old, it would change forever the way in which we live and the way in which we die.

Calvin, who had studied in or around the same time at the same school in Paris as Ignatius Loyola (which says something of interest to the nature–nurture argument) concluded that Adam and Eve had spent at most three hours during one late afternoon in the Garden of Eden between entrance and exit, nudity and nakedness, Creation and Fall. We think this quaint, and thereby miss the point by missing the poetry – by which I mean the terrible and necessary discernment of prosaic meaning, not pretty language – in his figure of speech. Calvin's commentary articulates a tragic anthropology in its vision of conflicted creatures who cannot be themselves because their primary desire is to be other than they are, to be originals and not copies, to be authentic and not second-hand; whose resentment undermines the whole of community in a deterministic chain reaction of accusation and counter-accusation that culminates in expulsion and murder as the principal hygienic régime of the human order, just as, in the plays and poems of an adjacent Mediterranean mythology, the preconscious prestige rivalry of Hellenic alphamales over a beautiful woman will inaugurate the inexorable funeral games of civilisation both in Troy's Asia Minor and in mainland Mycenaean Greece.

Evolution doesn't phase us any longer. The current pontiff was bunkered down in Castel Gandolfo only a fortnight ago with a team of seminarians, modelling a double helix of faith and science for future believers. Teilhard's eucharistic ecstasy at the sight of the splendour of a plural and polyverse creation set a fashion in the 1950s. Come to that, the Archbishop of Canterbury preached the sermon at Darwin's funeral service; and my own great-grandfather Alexander McHenry, both a geologist and a belt-and-braces Roman Catholic, combined a friendship with T.H. Huxley, Darwin's lieutenant, and a devotion to Our Lady that led him to call his home in Donnybrook, Maryville. The stardust in our individual skeletons, which is the glittering nuclear waste of the Big Bang, does not drive us to astonishment or adoration; and the forensic facts of our basic anatomy – that, as mystic John Moriarty has told us, 'we speak the Beatitudes through the incisors of a carnivore' – do not dumbfound us. The creationists, on the other hand, understand the dilemma well: for, if the Mesopotamian cosmology in Genesis surrenders to the exquisite physics of the third millennium, the entire scriptural project must become porous, problematic and poetic. Perhaps the resurrection itself is a parable and not a police report. For the poetic is strenuous, searching, unsettled. It makes the strange familiar, the familiar strange. It is the dialogue of loneliness and communion. It is word and breath, all gift and grace, a donation and not data.

Unlike most other early Near Eastern accounts of creation, Genesis is pacific. It shrinks from violence. Elohim, the gods, nominate the cosmos benignly. They name it into stable, serene, specific being, a vegetarian paradise at the centre of a masterpiece worthy of the structuralist Lévi-Strauss, and then they relinquish the same sacred task of entitlement to mankind. Utterance now becomes the normative act of the human. The office of saying is ours, genetically and generically. The Hebrew word 'nephesh', which means 'person', began by designating 'the throat', for behind this feast of naming in the Adamic account lies our species' ancient exhilaration at the bestowal of language as the birth of our differential identity in the world, just as the obsession with bread in semitic culture reflects a continuous thanksgiving across time for the accidental cross-pollination of two wild grasses whose hybrid produced wheat. Even our sister species, the Neanderthals whom we exterminated, lacked this privilege. They could communicate in a shorthanded, semaphoric manner with whimpers and whinnies, but these were vocalisations and not verbalisations.

If, however, we were born as homo sapiens sapiens into original sin, we were also born into original syntax. 'In the beginning was the Word', announces the heraldic high C of the fourth Gospel's opening phrase. A later Messianic Jew than John, Russia's revolutionary Leon Trotsky, would dispute the claim, insisting instead that 'In the beginning was the Deed, and the Word followed as its phonetic shadow'. But we know in our lungs and in our larynx that we are breath. We know it in the virtuoso vibration cycles of our vocal chords. Language is our earth and our ecosystem. To be sure, we are not the sinless stewards of any space, outer or inner or in-between. The only handwriting on the lunar surface so far is the signature of Richard Nixon; and the only voice travelling digitally through our solar system in a centrifugal capsule is, I gather, Kurt Waldheim's. But the love-cry of our kind, my mother's uninhibited sobbing not excepted, may send its tremolo far out and far away, as far indeed as the stars that are forming like tears in the foaming gases of the Horsehead Nebula.

Chapter Twenty-Four
WITNESS

ONLY THREE HOURS AGO the onset of sunset all over Ireland started the single most solemn fast in the Jewish calendar as the exquisite liturgy of the Day of Atonement (October 1–2) inaugurated the annual rites of Yom Kippur in the Dublin Orthodox synagogue. By then the same services had begun already in Sydney and in Singapore, Saint Petersburg and Budapest, and by midnight or the small hours here in our eastern Atlantic longitude the customary candle lighting ceremony will commence in Manhattan, Miami, Florida and Mexico City; wherever in fact, across countries and continents, the worldwide House of Jacob prepares prayerfully to recall the generous giving and forgiving of God in the second donation of the two stone tablets on the summit of Sinai. It's a period of repentance, of reflection, and of renewed moral resolve, a time of atonement in the traditional understanding of that expression, but also a time of at-onement with an unimaginable Lord who brought a victimised minority out of their internment camps in Egypt as a sign to the generations that Yahweh is the opposite of Pharaoh and not his transcendental archetype.

Just as, in the Jewish calendar, tonight is the ninth of Tishrei in the year 5767, so also, in the Islamic reckoning of the children of Ishmael who are newly Irish, this evening is the eighth of Ramadan, 1427. Like the memorial of Mount Sinai and the handing down from its heights of the Ten Commandments as an ethical epitome of community life, Ramadan also remembers a mystical transmission, the bestowal of the first verses of the Koran on the prophet Mohammed as the angel Gabriel reprises his appearance in the Book of Luke to announce the Word of God to the founder of the third Abrahamic faith; and so the entirety of the text of the Koran will be declaimed in the mosques during this lovely lunar season.

In Christianity, the intermediate revelation in the semitic trinity, it isn't such a calendrically hectic occasion, and, as titles go, I must acknowledge that the Twenty-Sixth Sunday in Ordinary Time doesn't have the snap, crackle and pop of its fraternal feasts and fasts in the other systems. Yet the lections selected for today's eucharists, one from the Hebrew Bible and one from the Gospel of Mark, do raise imposing questions about the rivalry and/or reciprocity between religions, and about the place of prophetic dissent within – and without – institutional ideologies. In the first reading from the eleventh chapter of Numbers (26-30), Joshua beseeches Moses to prevent two unaccredited prophets from practising without a licence. As Moses' aide-de-camp and eventual dauphin, Joshua is naturally and necessarily preoccupied by prestige, the pecking order, and the policing of any opposition. But Moses grandly rebukes his lieutenant: 'Would that all the people of the Lord were prophets,' he retorts. 'Would that the Lord might bestow his spirit upon them all!'

Much the same mise en scene recurs in the reading from Mark where this very sombre evangelist typically targets the preening inner circle of disciples. More id than ego, Jesus' immediate entourage, whose mood swings swerve in seconds from self-pity to self-importance, is infuriated to find out that some freelance fellow or other is claiming a connection with the bossman and carrying out charismatic cures in his name. This undermines their own status and seniority as the certified intimates of a celebrity, and status and seniority are what matter to men. But 'Do not prevent him,' Jesus admonishes the lot of them. 'For whoever is not against us is for us.' Whether as prophet or psychiatrist, in the parallel ministries of intellectual critique or therapeutic challenge (for the chap in Mark happens to be an exorcist), the testimony of the cultural and the counter-cultural witness cannot be limited to a shortlist of initiates, a register of the right types. It is an apostolate for all sorts and not the prerogative of any one college or creed. The holy spirit of the God of Jesus pollinates and cross-pollinates without regard to party membership; and this mention in Mark might well become a motto and a mantra for an Irish Church that is stricken with, and even addicted to, suspicion of the critical outsider. My own Roman Catholic community dreams discreetly of a future via media that would be more via than media, more evening prayer than *Evening Herald*; but if we cannot recognise the stranger as angel, in Saint Paul's expression, we can at least identify him as *angelos,* as messenger, and thereby honour the *euaggelion*, the 'good message' or the 'good news' as the Greek word calls the gospel.

Admittedly, the Christ of two later gospels says the very reverse in Luke 11 and Matthew 12, where, in a confessedly different setting, Jesus is credited with the comment, 'He who is not with me is against me'. By the same token, the narrative in the Book of Numbers continues in the next chapter with the stunning punishment of Moses' sister Miriam for presuming to compare her prophetic abilities with her much more famous sibling's. But the business of pitting one pericope against another pericope, one verse against another verse, advances little beyond the tedium of trumping in a card game. The truth is, religion has always been afraid of revelation, and, whether construed as simple prediction or as complex indictment, as social literature or as spiritual writ, prophetic utterance has always been closely patrolled by the Temple authorities. Compared to the smooth and sedimentary processes of a priestly cult, all smells and bells, the course of prophecy is igneous, an oxygenated flame. If the tabernacle of the Lord lay at the centre of the Israelite encampment in its long nomadic wandering through the wilderness, the oracle tent stood strategically outside it on the tolerated border; and if the closing sentences of Deuteronomy laud lawgiver Moses as the prophet par excellence – 'and there arose not a prophet since in Israel like unto him, whom the Lord knew face to face' – it is both to state the norm and to sound a warning to his restive and presumptuous posterity lest their aspirations become too boisterous.

In spite of the revisionist intentions of Tatian in the second century, we have inherited, thanks be to God, fully four gospels and not one. Equally, in spite of the heretic Marcion's simultaneous attempt to eradicate the Old Testament (so called) from the Christian library, our heritage encompasses the Pentateuch and the Prophets, those antiphonal volumes that Jesus of Nazareth studied for an ordinary lifetime before launching his mission to the marginalised of Israel. But the job of safeguarding the synod on Sinai or the Sermon on the Mount in Matthew's deliberately Mosaic account of it belongs to a very broad Church indeed, not just to the sacramentalists in their sanctuaries but to the sometime congregants and to the straightforward secularists as well; not just to those who break the bread officially but to those who wash the feet informally, not just to those who serve and steward within the walls but to everyone and anyone who witnesses to an ethic of magnanimous inclusion beyond all pettiness and vendetta. The late great Jesuit theologian Karl Rahner liked to invoke the multitudes of what he called 'anonymous Christians', non-affiliated persons without dogma or doctrine whose daily perseverance preserves the Judaic attitudes of non-violent outreach that Jesus modelled. So, when self-styled practising Christians insist that the use of church facilities be limited to those who are committed, and denied to those who are casual or occasional comers, a sort of sectarian arteriosclerosis informs the argument. White as snow is, after all, the biblical colour of leprosy; and an ancient *midrash* of the rabbis rightly reminds us that the Decalogue itself was given by God on Sinai in seventy languages, no less, Latin and Arabic among them.

As it happens, the synagogue service on Yom Kippur always privileges the blackly and bleakly comical novella about runaway prophet Jonah, a reluctant witness even by the standards of his easily panicked profession; and it also recites as its Torah portion the sixteenth chapter of the Book of Leviticus in which the luckless goat is driven as a proxy for the people's pollution into the inhospitable desert to die among demons. So the simultaneous starlight of a whole constellation of texts in Judaism and Judeo-Christianity illuminate in concert the themes of good riddance and of bad riddance, of advocacy and condemnation. For prophecy in the Hebrew Bible, the Bible on which Jesus ruminated as a literate artisan in Nazareth, always and everywhere points to what the Greeks described as 'tragedy' – *tragodos*, the road of the goat – in their theatrical classification of the innocent outcast who is criminalised as a culprit by a collective projection of loathing that thereby retrieves a semblance of social stability through the expulsion of those deemed alien. 'Scapegoat' would be translator William Tyndale's glittering coinage for this cultural category, but the Hebrew scriptures' scrutiny of the phenomenon could not prevent their future fate as a casualty of such conduct; for the pillar of cloud by day and the pillar of flame by night, that divine escort of the Exodus, would become in our own recent recollection the chimneys of the crematorium at Auschwitz.

'The Christian stands by God in God's hour of grieving', wrote Dietrich Bonhoeffer; and, God knows, there is grief enough to go round. Yet there are difficulties in the duty of the sentinel. The honour guard can turn into a gauntlet, bereavement into belligerence, and then the vicious circle of shaming and blaming, which is the hermeneutic circle of our civilisation, zeroes in again. The prophetic protest on behalf of the scapegoat can deteriorate into the scapegoating of the scapegoater. When the enabling love of the victim is a lesser thing than the energising hatred of the victimiser, we are no longer in the presence of the prophet but of the false prophet, which is to say the persecutor, the prosecutor, the pointed finger, against whom all the scriptures, Jewish and Jewish Christian, wisely warn us.

They might have cautioned us at the same time about our own culture, in which prophetic dissent is neutralised by swift absorption into the honours system and the prophylaxis of fame, to be regulated and regularised by rewards. In addition, Western liberal democracies have long since perfected the art of replenishing the rogues' gallery from generation to generation, from year to year, from weekday to weekend, so that the mythological bogeymen of bipolar politics, those rostered pariahs who fascinate us, inflame our fears, and fortify our sense of fellowship, whether they be Soviets, Shias, or local subversives, can go on guarding us from the sight and the plight of ourselves.

Chapter Twenty-Five
ASSUMING FLESH

THIS DAY LAST WEEK at the folk Mass in my parish church, I found I was rostered to read the first lesson, a rather mortifying rant against the rich in the letter of Saint James, the brother or step-brother of Jesus of Nazareth. As a credit card-carrying member of the dominant echelon, with two children, two cars, and two jobs, besides health insurance, holiday leave and pension plan, I belong to the single most rapacious species on the surface of the planet, worse in a way than any weapon of mass destruction, and that is the post-Enlightenment, European middle class male at work on his curriculum vitae in the smoke-without-fire of his vicious voodoo gods who can only proffer the past as achievement, the future as ambition, and the present as the place of prehensile excellence for the agile individual entrepreneur. Even so, I got up and read the thing with some attempt at gravitas. Fortunately, the whole harangue is aimed against others, against 'you rich' instead of 'we rich', so I was able to put my entire heart and soul into it. Being the reader also means you miss the first collection, which is great too.

Today's scriptural choices in the revised common lectionary feature a blinding binary star from Year B, combining the exquisite Yahwist fantasy of the creation of the first couple in Genesis 2 with the more litigious rabbinic wrangle over divorce in Mark 10. Roman Catholic laity get to proclaim the myth of our ancient nativity in the heart-breaking poetry of the Hebrew Bible; Anglican Catholic laity, being in this respect a luckier breed than their apostolic cousins, are invited to administer the gospel as well as the Old Testament lection, though the apparently hard-line logic of the transparently hard saying of Jesus in relation to relationships may not make this somewhat sticky section in Mark everybody's initial choice for a solo flight from the lectern.

On the other hand, the halcyon decency of the holiday in Eden when Adam's coma awoke his wife to the welcome world around her continues to this day generating in its wistful listeners an elegiac aftertaste of trust and tenderness. I remember reading it out loud myself, albeit in a miserable manner, in a previous parish life towards the close of the last millennium during a terrible time in my own marriage when, for whatever reason – either because I had stopped taking medication for manic depression or because, as young Americans say in a smashing phrase, 'shit happens' – I had begun to experience again, for the first time in almost ten years of solid quotidian sanity, delusions and dreadfulness of a kind that made for night terrors in broad daylight. One of my small children sat in a crowded front pew drinking effervescent orange squash from a plastic beaker and inhaling her maggoty scrap of a blanket while I broke the scripture in the sub-zero sanctuary. Sweat slipped down my sides under my shirt like the long metal chain of a religious medallion whose clasp had snapped at my Adam's apple. At any moment the shadow of a guard from the station in the street above would darken the door of the church to lead me away in disgrace as the praying shapes in the benches studied their leaflets in silence. Then my daughters could change their surnames to the Irish form of their mother's maiden name, and there would be peace of a kind, a peace amounting to kindness, in the promise of personal penal obliteration, the padded and the padlocked cells of my body closing in and closing down in their vile and stifling trillions.

All of which makes me wonder who in general might have recited the glittering alternative account of our bonded origins from the J version of Genesis this morning or evening in the gathered communities of church and chapel across the country? And who in particular might have made a nonsense of its opening line – 'The Lord God said, "It is not good for the man to be alone"' – by the daft substitution of the word 'person'? Certain of those who read it to their congregations must embody in their own partnerships and progeny the redemptive inner limits of its textual radiance, for happiness is no hallucination. We have all endured its impossible pain at some point. But among the tenor voices there are also countertenor cries, the cries of the liminal and the eliminated, of apartness and apartheid, of separateness and of separation. Perhaps the lesson was read by an older man in the little beatitude of a blundering second shot at wife and family after the mortgage and the meter readings of a prior public debacle. Perhaps it was read by a younger woman whose alcoholic husband swears and soils himself on the staircase in the small hours of their hidden ascension where the twelve steps have left no footprints yet on the thousand mile journey. Perhaps it was read by a twenty-something girl, the admonitory might of whose parents and psychotherapist put together cannot prevent from desiring a sweetheart of her own sex to the eligible escorts in the factory's health and fitness club where she has full membership. Perhaps it was even read by a child at a children's Mass, one whose parents must have consumed each other at some stage in the holy communion of their flesh and blood to bring him about, but who nowadays cannibalise each other like the dead mother of Odysseus in the underworld when she pretended to kiss her living offspring in order to wolf down the meat and cartilage of his facial mask.

'A man leaves his father and mother and clings to his wife, and the two of them become one flesh,' the text tells us.

('Clings', incidentally, translates the same Hebrew verb of utter attachment as the one used in the Book of Deuteronomy to define our radical closeness or 'cleaving' to God; and the idea of 'one flesh' includes and exceeds the image of coital completeness in the neat fit of heterosexual coupling to hint at real personal presence, at immeasurable mutuality, which is presumably part of what Jesus intended at the Last Supper when he spoke of the rendering and the rending of his body.) But the extrapolation from the idyllic and the ideal in Genesis to the prohibition of second marriages in the New Testament has always been problematic. On the one hand, the authenticity of Jesus' teaching is irrefutable. There is major and multiple attestation in Paul, in the gospels, and in the Q source of the scriptures, to the historical fact that he denounced divorce. Editorial smallprint in the very same sources, especially in Matthew's amendment and in Paul's epistolary pussyfooting, proves that from the primitive start of the Christian project the politbureau has had problems with the Master's directive. Jesus' own motives were typically impeccable. In a patriarchal culture that commodified wives and facilitated their effacement and replacement by a simple letter of severance, he was mindful of a minority – all women and all children without exception – whose marginality was also an actual statistical majority in the census of Judean society; and he sought always and everywhere to strengthen and safeguard them.

But the Lord was also an eschatological prophet of his tumultuous Judaic era who may well have believed that the world was about to end, and who wanted accordingly to revert to the primal purity of the dispositions in Genesis before the final in-breaking of the God of Israel. Additionally, he was speaking of marriage at a time and place when weddings were negotiated impersonally for the purposes of power, profit and prestige by extended family and not by the intended couple whose private considerations were neither here nor there. The business of exogamy, of trading and transferring females from household to household, is traditionally indifferent to individual inclination – so much so that *amour courtois* or courtly love, that late medieval literary convention in western Europe of a frank and feeling relationship between a man and a woman, assumes that any such factual experience of reciprocal desire must, by definition, be an adulterous one, since the state of wedlock was deemed almost automatically a state of deadlock as well.

The Priestly narrative in the first chapter of the Book of Genesis delays and defers the appearance of the human order until the sixth day of the week of God's inaugurating words in order to witness to our arrival as the crescendo and the climax of the divine act of imagination. The Yahwist stratagem in the parallel tradition of Genesis 2 reverses that series, foregrounding us instead as source rather than summit, the explosive starting point of Yahweh's heartfelt historical-pastoral-romantic-comical-tragical drama of his living images on earth. But both chronicles are chivalric genealogies, proclaiming us, each of us and all of us, to be the abiding passion of God, and rightly placing the pair-bond and the fecund future it gives rise to at the storm-centre of our travels in time-space towards the immensity of the meaning of the mystery.

In the record of creation that we read in the myth of Genesis, the provident Lord of the cosmos calls into being the whole structure and infrastructure of reality. He proceeds as a physicist, a chemist and a biologist, commencing and commending both the mineral order and the vegetable order. But he does not begin to bless the endeavour until the emergence of animal and then of animated life. Jesus extends that blessing in the Sermon on the Mount to those whom we wantonly misunderstand by translating the term 'blest' as 'happy'; for 'blessing' should communicate, as it does in modern French, an idiom of woundedness as well as welfare. So we cannot restrict that blessing to those who gratify the categories of canon law. It is our birthright as human agents. It is our battle cry. There is so much stress and distress in our being we must believe it becomes us. At times the surfeit of story and the dearth of plot can even suggest that Providence is a bad Booker novelist and not the love cry in the steaming breath of our language. Even the bereavement counsellors are bereft of counsel these times.

Yet the benediction in Genesis sanctifies all those, weak or strong, mainstream or marginal, legal or lawful, who pit their tiny and tremendous commitments against the grandiose animosities of a planet in conflict. The fragility of oneflesh and the sanity of our small relationships can oppose the gnostic propaganda of mass culture by confronting its gaseous generalities with the grit of the particular. They are the refugee tents of the covenant in contaminated territory, they are the unmarked house-churches of a city under curfew, they are dawn raids on the darkness; for 'we wrestle not against flesh and blood,' as Paul says in Ephesians, 'but against principalities, against powers, against the rulers of the darkness of the world, against spiritual wickedness in high places.'

Chapter Twenty-Six
'AFFLUENZA'

THE INDIVIDUAL who prostrates himself so publicly at Jesus' feet in today's reading from the Book of Mark (10:17-22) is truly three-dimensional, if only because each of the Synoptic gospels presents him differently. In that sense, as the collective image of a candidate for discipleship who displays an initial interest in the politics of poverty but who demonstrates eventual reluctance to relinquish anything, he may be said to represent an early Cubist composition by three quite distinctive Christian communities. The Markan portrait, which is the purest and most primitive of the four lives of Jesus in the New Testament, treats him as a wealthy personage and as something of a performer, perhaps even an exhibitionist. After all, by genuflecting he adopts a servile posture, more a Roman pose than a Jewish practice, the body language of the indentured and the enslaved instead of the manly face-to-face of Judaic culture. He is, in a word, moved and magnified by his own theatrical humility. Admittedly, Luke's later gospel will imagine Jesus as also kneeling down in the garden of Gethsemane, but that particular detail from the third passion narrative is meant to model a new liturgical rubric for Christian prayer groups that will thereby differentiate them from their alienated relatives in the synagogues who continue, in the ancient words of the Eucharistic hymn from the Mass of Paul VI, 'to stand in God's presence and serve him'. Matthew and Luke discreetly jettison the kneeling. Both are rightly embarrassed by it.

In addition, Matthew passes over the man's affluence in silence. His own membership of a sophisticated scribal constituency frequently encourages this evangelist to soft-pedal Jesus' historical strictness towards the respectably rich. There may indeed have been a contributing hardcore cadre of bourgeois believers in Matthew's circle whom it was prudent to appease. He therefore prefers to characterise the fellow first as simply 'someone' and then as 'a young man', excused by inexperience, lacking the longsightedness of age which will see, for example, the elderly scapegoaters repenting more readily than the adolescent stone-throwers in Saint John's story of the woman taken in adultery. Luke, on the other hand, identifies the wannabee recruit as a ruler, an 'archon', for the gentle gentile biographer of Jesus has been long enough in the world to understand the absolute reciprocity of power and pillage down through the ages to the present moment. 'What is to be done?' was, after all, the Lucan question par excellence long before it became a Marxist-Leninist mantra in our own time. Loot and licence belong together though the third millennium, much like the second one and the first before that again, incline to name simple cash and clout as income and influence, rank and reputation, or status and seniority. There are euphemisms aplenty for the fist.

In his heartless heart of hearts, the rich young ruler knows all of this. 'What must I do to inherit eternal life?' he asks the itinerant preacher, phrasing the task of authentic human growth in the jargon of commercial advantage; for the verb 'kléronomeó', to inherit, denotes the receipt of a share, the ownership of a portion, the possession of an object by an act of legal conveyance. In like manner, the complacent Jesuit priest in James Joyce's *Dubliners* will congratulate his mercantile congregation from the pulpit on having audited their moral accounts accurately before the approach of the Day of Judgement when their diligent double book keeping will deliver them from the censure of the heavenly Revenue Commissioners. Matthew's teasing revision of Mark's anecdote exaggerates the consumer crassness of the questioner, for, when Jesus suggests to him that he employ the commandments as an ethical nucleus of humane conduct, the chap retorts with a tart business interrogation: 'Which ones?' This is, after all, market-share morality. He doesn't wish to produce merchandise he can't sell. He doesn't want to invest time or attention in any entrepreneurial endeavour without a guaranteed percentile return within a specified period.

Little wonder that his literal enthusiasm – enthusiasm meaning, as it does in Greek, 'the god within us' – peters out. At the start of the story, he has called Jesus a 'good teacher', 'didaskale agathe'. At the mid-point, he again addresses him but this time only as 'teacher', 'didaskale', since Jesus is no longer earning his meritorious adjective; and, at the end of the encounter, he will call him nothing at all, because by now Jesus is, as it were, all Greek to the party of the first part. There is no word in the rich man's vernacular for what this strange person from the bogs of Galilee signifies. If it be the case that we belong first and foremost to our own deepest longings, then this posh plutocrat longs for, and belongs to, the activity of possessiveness because he mistakes it, in a capital error, for the act of self-possession. He has been defiled not by his vices but by his virtues, and the defilement consists in the fact that those virtues have degenerated into mere virtuosity. Ironically, he has defrauded someone, and that someone he has short-changed is himself. Unlike the little children of the immediately preceding sections of Mark's gospel, he cannot quit his permanent fortifications for the green ecosystem of perfect trust that the kids typify as the small royalty of God's kingdom. He cannot practise dying, and to practise dying is eternal life. It is only as transients and as aliens, as the trustees of our existence and not as the bailiffs of our lives, that we can earth ourselves and take root in the here and now as real presences.

The scandalous nature of the reading of the rich young man in Mark shifts sideways seismically from time to time and from culture to culture. Matthew, who edited it early on in the first century, was primarily appalled by his predecessor's apparent disavowal of Jesus' divinity. 'Why do you call me good?' Mark reports the Master as saying. 'No-one is good but God alone.' This is an indiscretion amounting to a difficulty, and we may therefore be sure that Jesus said it. If the words were not his *ipsissima verba*, his own particular articulation as certified by the apostolic tradition, the embryonic Christian clusters in the eastern Mediterranean would ruthlessly have suppressed them, as they moved in a matter of decades beyond the conventions of Judaic monotheism with its entirely human Messiah to proclaiming the supernatural station of a pre-existent saviour at the right hand of God.

But the contemporary scandal of the story has to subsist in its peculiar poetics of emptiness, more Zen than Amen. After all, prosperity in the biblical imagination generally signals God's glad acknowledgment of our goodness, while deformity of circumstance – poverty, sickness, misadventure – can point to the punishment of some undisclosed viciousness or other behind the veil of our seeming sincerity. Moreover, the rabbinic consensus tends to condemn extravagant giving as a form of charity that extorts ovations by self-advertisement, and imperils personal responsibility for one's own welfare. Even today, in the Protestant and Puritan vocabulary of American cinema, restoration to prestige and to privilege is both the destination and the destiny of happy-ever-after Hollywood. Films about failure belly flop badly. And at this time of year especially, this damp, deciduous season, when we stock and store the pantry, prepare and provision the heaped harvest festival of the Fall for the sterile winter ahead of us, surely it makes less sense than ever to let go and to let be, to parrot this rhetoric of elective poverty – for the unelected kind is, we must always remind ourselves, intrinsically evil.

If the Irish middle classes were fascinated to the point of obsession by the fin de siecle presidency of Mary Robinson, it was partly because her incumbency revived in their ranks the latent bourgeois fantasy, which the late Archbishop John Charles McQuaid also projected as a Catholic magnate in my infancy, that glamour and the gospel can go together, that power and piety are accomplices and not adversaries, that the life of grace and gracious living can exchange the sign of peace, and that the Mass at which the handshake happens is only beautiful. Plato knew this to be nonsense five hundred years before Christ tunnelled his way down the birth canal in live-stream Bethlehem. Only our brokenness can construct us now. In the steadily subtracting light of middle and late life, our ruins look like scaffolding, our scaffolding like ruins. If we do not live under the sign of that double fragility, we depart like the man in Mark with our stubborn portfolios, our letters of reference, the deadly, leaden credentials after our name.

For the sake of the story that's in it, I could call that grieving, gone-away figure by name. I could call him Alexander McHenry, Sandor Ben Someone or other in the Hebrew form, an ambitious, amassing great-grandfather of mine who survives today in the aftermath of his alpha-malehood as a dented silver snuffbox without a lid to it, where my daughters kept their canines for the Tooth Fairy once upon a time, a long time ago. I could call him by my own name, Aidan Mathews, a man who learned three words in the dictionary each day for ten years from seven to seventeen in a desperate attempt to impress his peers and his parents, who were the lofty proxies of God, and to manipulate his world more profitably, but whose later sabbaticals in bedlam brought him the gifts of speechlessness. If he had made it as a boy to the letter T, the twentieth of the English alphabet, the nineteenth in the Latin language, and the last of all in the oldest lists of the Greek letters from the first Phoenician originals, that same Aidan Mathews might someday have sounded the word Thesaurus with the tip of his tongue on the dry roof of his palate. 'Thesaurus'. For it is precisely 'thesaurus', in English 'treasure', that Jesus, the bilingual Galilean, offers the rich young ruler. It is 'thesaurus en ouranó', treasure in heaven, by which the Lord doesn't intend some ultimate vaporous dividend in the cumulonimbus of the clouds but a prophetic commitment to the precious little of life as the proper produce of eternity.

Thirty years ago I sat in a Cretan cemetery in the city of Iraklion reciting over and over the inscription on a famous headstone in front of me. 'Den elpizo tipote; den phobomai tipote; eimai lephtheros.' 'I hope for nothing. I am afraid of nothing. I am a free man.' It's a farewell with flair from novelist Nikos Zazantzakis, as much a trencherman as his own zestful Zorba the Greek and neither rich nor a ruler nor remotely young when he said it. Thirty years on, I may have more time for hope as our hard, scarred orientation. But the link between freedom and fearlessness is still worth making. It is more than a secular assertion, more even than the high clamour of humanism. It is the gospel truth.

Chapter Twenty-Seven
RANSOM NOTES

I FINISHED UP LAST WEEK by admitting to an addictive liking for dictionaries and the intricate clarity of their anatomical contents. The recitation of linked word lists, the musical concatenation of their roots and branches up and down the pages of the OED, which was the only volume in my home that was as heavy and as perfumed as the Bible, gratified some primitive piety in me, and I would chant the tiny columns aloud like the litany of Our Lady's titles in a Marian canticle, with a simple, sensual contentment, in the kind and radiant woodland of my dad's deciduous library. Milton maintains in one or other of his essays that Anglo-Saxon sorts can't speak a continental language, especially the Romance ones, because they're too inhibited to make such erotic shapes with their lips, and, right enough, I'm limited to the English language as my ultimate nationality, but that hasn't stopped me fibbing down through the years by filling out my bookshelves with impressive works like Liddell and Scott's celebrated *Greek-English Lexicon*, where I'm looking now, on page 481, at a particular word and its principal meaning, because its presence in today's reading from Mark may be said to have made a lot of mischief over many centuries in and through the counter-cultural process that we call Christianity.

The word is 'lutron', and in a double sense. On the one hand, the Greek noun means a 'ransom' or 'ransom money', not only in classical texts by Herodotus and Thucydides, but also in the semitic scriptures of the much later New Testament where both Mark and his successor Matthew attribute to Jesus the private revelation to his disciples that he had come to give his life as a ransom for many. On the other hand, the word is 'lutron' also, insofar as that equation of one with the other achieves a sort of theological epitome, the digest of a dogma. The Word of God, the incarnate Logos, the second person of the Blessed Trinity, ransoms and redeems us by his death on the cross. In this bizarre version (or possible perversion) of Christian anthropology, we are seen as a sorry species, the more so for not being sufficiently sorry at all, imbued as it were from our aboriginal outset with such sheer stamina of sinfulness that the mortified deity who made us demands requital but decides to deflects his homicidal wrath, through some quirky increment of eternal pity, from the proper target of his thirst for satisfaction, upon the substitutionary holocaust of the crucifixion of the Son by a sacrificial act of supernatural self-harming.

This grim gibberish, this intellectually despicable doctrine, has enjoyed what we have had to endure, a versatile and profiteering history. To be sure, it figures as one single, if very singular, reading of the death of Jesus among a plurality of possible interpretations, but its dominion in devotional life and in the sphere of sacrificial thinking has given it supremacy of status. Like an ingenious virus whose many mutations enable it always to stay one step ahead of every intended antidote, it has survived intact all the schismatic and secessionist squabbles of the Christian community over two Western millennia, and its deluded doctrinal vitality continues to romp through the Roman and Reform traditions of faith; but, at bottom, its thinking is every bit as blinkered and as cold-bloodedly clinical as high priest Joseph Caiaphas' politic preference that one man should die for the sake of the nation. 'The Kingdom of Heaven has suffered violence, and the violent take it by force', says the Jesus of Matthew in his encomium of his assassinated cousin, the

Baptist; but the same could be said to be true of the cross of Christ itself which has suffered for centuries the abysmal violence of the theology of atonement, a lethal medieval interpretation of the state killing on Calvary that substitutes a macabre and idolatrous model of God's compensatory vengefulness for the divinely non-violent unveiling of the evil, exclusionary acts that constitute the human polity.

Not that I'd ever heard of the eleventh-century Saint Anselm of Canterbury, the episcopal author of truly hardcore atonement theory, when I was a first communicant with a fistful of broken crayons colouring the black-and-white illustrations in my catechism in the pre-conciliar Church of Trent, or that I should scapegoat the poor man now for having harped, in one impenetrable portion of his prolific reflections, on the necessary juridical murder of Jesus through the agency of a supposedly satanic Sanhedrin. Besides, there were lucid voices in my early vicinity that pitted themselves against this ludicrous, legalistic exegesis of the passion, and they were mostly the voices of the Jesuits who taught me in the 1960s; for, in the complexities of modern Irish life, if not always in the simplicities of modern Irish literature, priest and prophet can be synonyms and not asymmetrical opposites. These several men, peace be upon them, instructed me to read everything on the Index of Prohibited Books if I wanted to be in any way adequate to the world that awaited me outside the sight lines of the school grounds. Behind the Johannine Lord of the fourth gospel, a text considered vexing and heterodox by the early Church, they showed me the seditious synoptic Jesus who scandalised the sincerely religious authorities of his age, just as the same dissenting presence would be anathematised and excommunicated in our own era by a careful and conscientious Curia. Beyond the Christ who choreographs his own cultic execution as a celestial dramaturge in the book of John, these men of the second council could discern an innocent casualty transformed by the filter of men's fearfulness into a culprit and a criminal in order to function effectively for them as a scapegoat for the sake of so-called stability in a civil society that would not and could not candidly acknowledge, any more than ours will, its deep, daily, and habitual reliance on violence to sustain itself.

For this is how Jesus bears/bares our sins, not by 'bearing' them as a porter or a sort of transport, as a conveyance or conduit that carries them away conveniently from those who committed the offences in the first place, but by 'baring' our sinfulness in the sense of exposing and exhibiting it to sight and to scrutiny by an act of literal apocalypse. For the word 'apocalypse' means an uncovering, a disclosure, a stripping naked, a laying bare, and that is precisely what the Passion narratives in the New Testament do: they uncover, they disclose, they strip naked, and they lay bare the brutal genesis and the bloody ground of human community that we camouflage so grandiosely in the golden language of law and order, of compact and contract, in the Greek and Latin abracadabra of our sanitised, statutory, sacrificial ziggurats. Our hospitality towards our fellows is premised on our hostility towards our foes. For we do not unite together: we unite together against. There is no neighbour without a neighbourhood; and there is no neighbourhood without Neighbourhood Watch, without the watch towers and the barbed wire, because there be monsters in our midst and on our borders, and things that go bump in the night.

In my formative and deforming years, between my state as an altar boy and the stage of late adolescence, I could observe many of my own generation abandoning Anselm's ideology of atonement as unintelligible drivel – and a blasphemy to boot against the pacific and paternal Yahweh whom Jesus encountered in the mild privilege of the Judaism he was born to. The remainder, myself included, internalised its drastic ethos of ritualistic victimisation until the whole and holy universe was diminished to the size of an exercise yard, a sphere of perfect surveillance, a tortuous, transparent place of exaction and penalty, prescript and proscript, requiring in turn a Mother Church no less preoccupied with the statistics of sacrificial propitiation through the magical misuse of the sacraments than the Temple cult that Christ despised two thousand years ago. In the process, faith degenerated into mere fatalism, and the enterprise of ethical risk, which is solidarity with the solitude of God as the true outcast of creation, was degraded to the meagre level of routine moral arithmetic. From being a sanctuary and a safe house for the vilified of the world, the Church sank down and subsided into a secular anchorage of high art. The hermit's place grew into the Hermitage in Leningrad. Indeed, from the moment that the deacon became a lesser person than the priest, from the time that the ceremony of the cult overshadowed the service of the vulnerable, the writing was on the wall; and the writing on the wall said: This Church is now a National Heritage Monument.

For the faith can survive culture only by remaining outside culture, despite all the blandishments of the fashion that would match it to the modes of the moment. It is, by its very nature, counter-cultural, an irony that cannot be quarantined, mockery of the dead centre from the live margins. Its only chain of office is to be in chains for the sake of the gospel and of the great good news of the Judaism that birthed the gospel. The Bible, both in the wealth of its Hebrew witness and in the Jewish Christian writings, records an extraordinary Middle Eastern conversation over many centuries, from the Middle Bronze Age to late antiquity, between retaliation and reconciliation, force and forgiveness. It begins in myth and ends in history, describing thereby an ever increasing contour of clarification as to what we are and what we do as creatures in conflict. It starts with the mythical expulsion of men and women by a maddened God and it ends with the historical expulsion of an envoy of God's love by maddened men and women. By so doing, it eventually intuits the utter non-violence of the Creator whom we have defined so slanderously in our own image and likeness.

In today's reading from Mark, James and John, the sons of Zebedee, pester Jesus for promotion and perks. They want to sit one at his right and the other at his left in a visible vantage where they can admire themselves in the mirror of general resentment by the other disciples. Matthew, who can be priggish about apostolic dignity when he chooses, scapegoats their unfortunate mother instead, alleging that she's an upwardly mobile matron, and the boys themselves are blameless. The love of our children does bring out the worst in us, which may be why the New Testament is so hard on family life. But everybody in the story has missed the point, for the honour guard of the Lord will not be drawn from any inner circle. Instead, it will be two condemned criminals, the anonymous jetsam of history, who will stand beside him in the place of human judgement.

Chapter Twenty-Eight
REVISIONARIES

TODAY'S GOSPEL from the Book of Mark (10:46-52) is short enough to be quoted in full. It reports the healing of a blind man on the outskirts of Jericho as Jesus and his footsore entourage steer finally for Jerusalem and the feast of Passover. I give it in the Authorised Version since I don't have to clear copyright on a seventeenth-century translation of the text, and also because I love its archaic darkness of diction, which was much criticised even at the time by its earliest Anglican audiences for its opportunistic mimicry of already fake and old-fashioned language to give it, I suppose, a patriarchal patina, the gravitas of a grey-haired hauteur. Here it is, anyway.

> As Jesus went out of Jericho with his disciples and a great number of people, blind Bartimaeus, the son of Timaeus, sat by the highway side, begging. And when he heard that it was Jesus of Nazareth, he began to cry out and say 'Jesus, thou son of David, have mercy on me.' And many charged him, that he should hold his peace; but he cried the more a great deal, 'Thou son of David, have mercy on me.' And Jesus stood still, and commanded him to be called: and they call the blind man, saying unto him, 'Be of good comfort, rise, he calleth thee.' And he, casting away his garment, rose and came to Jesus. And Jesus answered, and said unto him,

'What wilt thou that I should do unto thee?' The blind man said unto him, 'Lord, that I might receive my sight.' And Jesus said unto him, 'Go thy way, thy faith hath made thee whole': and immediately he received his sight, and followed Jesus in the way.

There are many Markan habits at work in this pericope. The evangelist's characteristic pleasure in the word 'immediately' is one such, because he loves the drama of sudden disclosure and the moment of human decision as a defining act that is central to our dignity. His preference for the phrase 'the Way' and 'on the Way', not as a road sign or a toll for traffic but as a pedestrian idiom of pilgrimage and the proper imitation of Jesus, is another – so much so indeed that the whole Christian project became known throughout the Greek-speaking Eastern Mediterranean within a generation of Jesus' death by this shorthand term, this password, this plenary reference to travel as travail and travail as travel. And a third typical tactic of the oldest gospel we possess is the metaphoric use of the casting off of clothes – which Saint Francis would interpret very literally a millennium later when he stripped before his father – as a recurrent figure of speech to describe the snake-like shedding of a skin in due season, our ability to moult the stiff fixity of the past in order to mould a supple future: in brief new life, rejuvenation, a turning, the necessary crisis of all choice at any crossroads. More generally, the theme of blindness and enlightenment, of blinkers and inklings, of insight and hindsight, is the crucial and excruciating core of this entire section of Mark's testimony in which sightless persons are always seen, topsy-turvy style, to be more discerning than the speculative seers who cannot glimpse the visionary sodality of Skid Row.

But the problem we experience in approaching this episode of the pretty prompt healing of a major handicap by a holy man en route to his immolation isn't eased by the sage small print of the paperback scholars I'm trying to remember more or less accurately from a brief browse. The ratio of actual true-life incident to active theological content in the paragraph about Bartimaeus isn't the real quandary, either. Whether or not it took place in reality is secondary to whether or not it takes root in its readers. Is it a documented eyewitness account or is it a doctrinal thumbnail, a catechetical nutshell? What it means to us today is what matters most, and what matters here is, inter alia, that its first-century message is no longer visible to the modern eye precisely because of the eventual victory of Christianity over superstition and the evil eye; for, in the two thousand years of its slow seepage into the substrate of Western consciousness, the Christian perspective on suffering, amounting almost to a mythology of victimhood, has so altered the cultural construction of anguish that affliction is now regarded as a badge of prestige instead of a proof of impurity and pollution, as it was in Jesus' time, when Bartimaeus, dodging the diabolical crowd, ingratiated himself with the famous faith healer, using words that still feature in the Kyrie Eleison of the penitential rite. For physical suffering, in particular, registers nowadays as spiritual stigmata rather than as social stigma, which was its primary Palestinian import in a culture where the sociology of reputation dwarfed the science of cures.

Yesterday's welts, in other words, have become today's epaulettes. Our weeping wounds, our scar tissue, the surgical strikes of our non-elective sorrows, are worn on the chest like regimental rewards, as the glittering certificate of our superior spirituality. Our version of the trek to Mecca takes the form of the hajj to Lourdes. We privilege grief as the shadow of the Holy Spirit's presence. If Judaism extols the valor of God, the Jesus cult exalts God's vulnerability. But this is, in a sense, a Christian fetish which reverses and inverts the standard biblical fashion for full health as God's public measure of our moral merit. After all, the word for 'health' and 'salvation' is one and the same in Latin, and the Latin Church of my own tradition continued this primitive double-think up to well within living memory, since a candidate presenting for clerical ordination could not be disabled or defective in any way whatsoever.

The Greek meaning of Bartimaeus is 'Son of Honour'. This is ironic, since Bartimaeus has been made dishonourable by sickness, much in the manner that mental illness or a sexually transmitted disease elicits a short and slimline sympathy from those who like to lavish solicitude on strokes and cancers. So the beggar's blindness is no mystical connection with the paschal mystery of the Passion of Christ, but an outcast state, the consequence of a community verdict of automatic ejection and rejection. Medicine in his world, being a branch of moral theology rather than a therapeutic science, would estimate his condition in ethical and not in ophthalmalogical terms, from a Gnostic and not a diagnostic viewpoint. In this reading of his infirmity, the man is a sinister and sinful alien, not the patient patient of our contemporary stereotype in which fortitude, the last refuge of a taste for fatalism, consecrates our calamities. How would Bartimaeus elucidate my neurasthenic infancy, forty years ago, where a local thalidomide child would be so cherished by the whole parish that a few of his able-bodied contemporaries, myself among them, dreamed of a similar deficiency to make us whole and holy for once in the stern eyes of all those adults, priests and parents, who otherwise withheld or withdrew their glance of blessing, their gaze of benediction? And how would Bartimaeus illuminate the strangely masochistic fantasies I devised, long before puberty enlarged my libido, to soften the cinder path from insomnia to sleepiness? For those deliberate dreams cross-pollinated Michelangelo's 'Pieta', the corporal punishment of my prep-school regime, and the beautiful bee-stung lips of Francoise Hardy, a mid-60s chanteuse, to produce a moist scenario in which, having been tortured ingeniously to the point of death by the Gestapo, I gave up the ghost while being breastfed by a tearful, if rather tarty, member of the French Resistance whose post-War wardrobe always incorporated the leather jacket and winkle-picker shoes from the sleeve of a vinyl LP called, appropriately enough, 'L'Amour d'un garcon'.

A twelve-year-old classmate who had informed me a couple of Christmases before that Santa was a fiction went on to read me the facts of life as I neared thirteen. To make it a hateful hat trick, it was he who pointed out to me in the fullness of time at a Young Scientists' Exhibition in Ballsbridge that the man who was blind from birth in the ninth chapter of Saint John wouldn't have been able to see anything apart from a chaos of colour until weeks and weeks after his so-called cure when his retina stabilised sufficiently to begin to shape the sights it was seeing, and the same or something similar would be no less true of the beggar Bartimaeus in the white dust of the royal road to Jerusalem. But I didn't need this particular positivist in Senior Three to start me wondering. In a remote corner of the country, I had seen a woman prise her false eye out of her face and suck it like a boiled sweet. I had watched congas of little kids crossing to the corner shop at the zebra outside the gates of the Blind Asylum on the Merrion Road in Dublin, with their taller albino chaperones at the top and tail of the silent, shuffling queue, like the mustard gas casualties of my granduncle's regiment in the Great War. Only two months ago, for that matter, in the Impressionist rooms in the Musée d'Orsay in Paris, I saw an elderly blind man with a collapsible white stick fiddling with the ear phones of his audio guide as he rotated slowly in a whispering space that was full of Edgar Dégas' pastel dancers on tiptoe in their rustling tutus round him. How might such a person listen to the scripture lessons of the lame leaping and the dumb speaking and the sightless seeing again in the prophetic ecstasies of the Israelites? Would he be scandalised by the false profligacy of the promises of God? How much metaphor could he be asked to endure in his vigil without night lights?

'I know' and 'I have seen' are the same word in Ancient Greek, where men believed their eyes and became rational by looking at everything except the sun. Philo the Jew, Jesus' great Alexandrian contemporary, was so impressed by the primacy of vision that he wanted to revisit the entirety of the Hebrew Bible, altering its acoustical diction from the vocabulary of saying and hearing to that of seeing and showing. But Bartimaeus doesn't want to be Aristotle's pupil. He's a Jew and not an Athenian. He wants his sight back because he wants his status back. Banishment and not blindness is the problem, just as the shame and infamy of crucifixion mattered infinitely more to the first Christians than any physical distress that Jesus may or may not have suffered in the process of being hanged. So Jesus' question, 'What do you wish that I shall do for you?' – the very same question posed a page earlier to James and John when those two very blind men came foraging for honoraria – is more concerned with the cultural glaucoma that excludes the handicapped than with the physiology of Bartimaeus' affliction, and the beggar, whose real desire is to stand in the light of ultimate acceptance, is immediately absorbed into the rag, tag and bobtail fellowship of the Lord's followers.

Chapter Twenty-Nine
THE FEAR OF GOD

IN TODAY'S FIRST READING from the Book of Deuteronomy in the Hebrew Bible, the prophet Moses exhorts the Israelites to 'fear the Lord, your God' (13:4). The response to the accompanying psalm, which boasts in its biblical way of carnage and conquest, converts such awe into affection with the victor's exhilarated declaration, 'I love you, Lord, my strength', while the gospel of the day rehearses the historical Jesus' absolute insistence on that love of the Lord as our primary pious impulse. Indeed all three synoptic evangelists hammer home the same imperative in a manner that struck me at a certain stage in my teenage years as somewhat terrible, in the elderly sense of the term: we must love God, they tell us, with an exclusive eagerness, with heart, soul, strength and intellect combined, in a concentration of attentiveness that might be mistaken for monomania.

It's a daunting agenda, this, and from childhood I had difficulties with it. The fear of God I understood well enough from Montessori onwards, though by that I don't for a moment mean that I had the kind of intimidated infancy which occurs as a colourless literary convention in endless Irish novels where the undivided individual heroically resists the psychotic atrocities of his priest-ridden society in order to emerge later on as a martyr if not as a celebrity and even a cult figure. No. What the fear of God signified in its old-fashioned form in my schooldays was a curiosity about the Creation and God's vivid complicity with it, the whole of the pollinating cosmos without and within me, from starbursts to bloodstains, from the iconostasis of the night sky over the city to the sacristy of its dirty, fertile streets, because this curiosity hurtled us in an accelerating spiral from interest to infatuation, from infatuation to rapture, and from rapture to awe. God left us open-mouthed, and it was only then, in the startled parting of our lips, that we could begin to proclaim his praise.

The curriculum's changed in the meantime, of course. Classroom Christianity since the Second Vatican Council has back-pedalled considerably on the Byzantine majesty of the inscrutable source of all being, preferring to fast-forward to the Latin leniencies of God's intentions toward humanity as laid out meticulously in the life, death and vindication of the victimised Jesus of Nazareth. But this semi-domestication of the mystery of God isn't the whole story or, for those who aren't Christian, the last word, either. One of the great potential gifts of Islam to the community of the Incarnation may well be the purity of its prostration before the unutterable strangeness of God, a posture we, with our Catholic laxity, are in danger of prescinding from, at times criminally, through the serene perils of our very sense of proximity. Images too may be idols, for, as Meister Eckhard reminds us, 'If God is to enter, the creature must leave', a timely caution that came to mind when a friend of mine, facing serious surgery, handed to a nurse in the ante-room of the operating theatre not only his credit cards but his immaculate medal of Mary as well. Nakedness, after all, is the norm of certain ultimate encounters.

So much for the fear of God understood, in the climax of its courtship, as the surprise of sudden shyness before the Beloved. But what of the love of God misunderstood as the onus of sheer obligation, as a forced fidelity? How could love be a command performance? How could we be constrained to commit a voluntary act? The default deity of the 1950s was, in my remote memory of him, all magistrate and no mercy, but the problem of approaching the bench in a church that copied a procedural court system was superbly side-stepped by a compex culture of client and patron, of serial and systematic intercession. The Father could be accessed through the Son, the Son through his mother, and the mother through a myriad of saints in a pell-mell, petitionary free-for-all that largely reproduced the cronyism and brown paper bag baksheesh of the Republic in which it occurred. As a pupil in a Jesuit college, I was a protégé of Ignatius Loyola, the sex and violence of whose early life endeared him to me, although I think I preferred several of his brothers in the Basque badlands, starting with the one who had swashbuckled his way through Mexico with General Cortez, then quartering for a period with another one who had slaughtered Muslim enemies on Europe's mutinous eastern borders, and finally and forever championing the stay-at-home sibling, a forgotten parish priest who probably did his level best, sanctified the nondescript precincts in which he found himself by a lifetime's ordinary service, loved his common law wife, filled the village with her illegitimate offspring, and died on his mattress in a matter of fact fashion, a Sancho Panza with the dignity of a Don Quixote. Life has made me a practising imperfectionist, and I admire this country curate more even than his canonised counterpart whose much later Jesuit companions, at the fag-end of the second millennium, would attempt to teach me Pass Irish, Honours Latin and general Religious Knowledge before the syllabus of that last subject withered into Civics and sex instruction in the 1970s.

Thirty years on, I'm still quicker at the third declension than the Módh Coiníollach. As for the love of God, I've learned through the double helix of luck and fiasco that the initiative, here as in everything else, resides with Providence and not with the person. We love by imitation and by example, or we do not love at all – which is to say, in a wry reversal of our vertical vainglory, that the other precedes the self and inaugurates it, that our nature is therefore second nature, a slow, derived learning and not a singular disclosure, a rich receptivity and not the eureka moment of the stark ego. Hominised in the womb and humanised in the commune, we are the perfect copy of what originates us. Jesus was grounded in the love of a God whom he conceived of, by the power of the spirit, as a father and familiar presence. The Judaism which fed and watered his faith in that fatherhood was itself founded not on metaphysical expertise through Socratic quizzing but on a people's physical experience of being cherished and chosen and intimately minded through the sorties and the detours of history, in Exodus and in exile.

When, accordingly, he answers the scribe's question about which precept has primacy, Jesus does so as an orthodox interpreter of Torah – for the English 'law' translates 'torah' as clumsily as 'word' translates 'logos' – by dovetailing texts from Deuteronomy and from Leviticus to present the mutuality of the two grand commandments to love God and love neighbour. This is a routine rabbinic response to the overwhelming question of what action best embodies us. The Jewish sensibility has always enjoyed succinctness, and, just as a modern particle physicist has inscribed the text of the Shema, Judaism's credo, on a single molecule of carbon with the laser nib of an electron microscope, so Jesus might have said in the expression of the sage Hillel who was his Palestinian contemporary: 'This is the whole Law. The rest is only commentary.' To be sure, the neighbour in the Book of Leviticus implies a fellow Jew and not a Gentile alien, but the first Jewish Christians would extend the fraternal franchise universally to all outsiders in the name of their assassinated founder – which is why, I imagine, Luke concludes the dialogue with the searching scribe by having Jesus tell him the story of the good Samaritan.

Christianity is a minority reading of the Jewish scriptures in which Davidic expectations are replaced by the thematics of a martyric Messiah. Within Christianity itself are many mansions, some of which are incompatible. The god of Armageddon, for example, whom so many evangelical Christians in North America sincerely proclaim is incompatible with the god of armistice in my own tradition. Yet, because I was born in the 1950s, I am the beneficiary of at least two distinguishable Christianities, the first of which encouraged contempt of the world – the so-called 'fuga mundi' – and the second of which encouraged passionate social and political commitment to it. My mother worried more about my soul than about my body; my daughters fret over my breathing, not my core beliefs. Up to the age of fifteen, I never heard a sermon on social justice; and, since the age of thirty-five, I haven't heard a homily on personal sin. When I was small, sexual unhappiness was as common as chest infections, prudishness and prurience were spellbound synonyms in this state, and the tidy towns of Ireland, all Kill and Cull, huddled over an ugly obsession with continence, until the lot of us seemed like the prostitutes in Renaissance Florence who were forced by their city fathers to wear their clothing inside out as a mark of their office, with their underwear outside their overcoats. Now, forty years on, the body's as banal as any mannequin, a streamlined, silicone instrument, more template than temple, expressionless from the paralysing toxins of Botox.

Times change, and we change with them; yet we know in our depths and in our shallows that anachronism too can be ahead of its time. So the desire and the duty to love God mindfully, wholeheartedly, willingly and wilfully, with brains and brawn, shrewdness and sinew together, is also and always a straightforward summons to discern the one revealed Lord, the only God of Israel, the dear Father of Jesus, amid the dizzying line-up of all the impromptu polystyrene substitutes we strew around our sanctuaries: the idols, the voodoo masks, the sectarian caricatures, the puritan god, the partisan god, the party-political god, the regurgitated god of our own internal curfew and censorship. Joy in the true God, joy in the true God's reconciling, non-violent, loving-kindness, cannot be confused with the emotion of elation. The moronic grin on the face of the charismatic should flinch and should fade away before the features of the crucified, for life is very serious and very stressful and very distressed, not least because most of us have been crucifiers as well as casualties. We have not chosen the enigmatic smile of the Buddha as a key to detachment, but the death mask of the human victim as a clue to God's heartbreak within history.

Chapter Thirty
SCRIBBLERS

WHEN I STUDIED in the States a quarter century ago, one of my teachers was the scholar Ian Watt, a serene, chain-smoking sage best known to generations of grateful Eng. Lit. undergraduates as the author of a ground-breaking reflection on the rise of the novel as a formal category in the mercantile and individualist era of the Williamite settlement in sixteenth- and seventeenth-century England. In the age of the Xerox photocopier, his stuff had been cogged from Cambridge to Canberra and back again; but the demobbed don who had endured the war years as a skeletal POW in a Japanese camp on the River Kwai was quite benevolent about this plagiarism. He had learned to be a Buddhist in captivity, when he used to help some Benedictine fellow inmates to make sufficient spit-balls of altar wine for their Eucharists in return for a proportion of their roll-your-own tobacco allowance from the occasional Red Cross consignment. Unfortunately, the good fathers could provide no cigarette paper to wrap the weed, so Professor Watt was obliged to smoke Dante's *Divine Comedy* in the original terza rima, since that was the only book he could buy or barter for, with the right kind of thin, translucent pages. He inhaled the flames of the Inferno and the rays of the Purgatorio, and he was half-way through the high-frequency light of the Paradiso when the atom bomb incinerated the Roman Catholic city of Nagasaki and another war, less chilling because colder, started up in the scorched earth and the salted fields of Central Europe. It was still going on, forty years later, when I heard the story from his own lips and their bobbing non-filter fag-end, and, even then, in the hedonistic haze of Northern California, he was able to recite the whole of Italy's masterpiece, bar the last couple of cantos, because he had felt, in the period of his imprisonment, that he wasn't ethically entitled to burn the book unless he first committed its contents to memory.

I understood this respect for texts, if only because the practise had mutated in my indigenous Irish culture into a sort of reverence, however wary and wry, for writers as well as their writings. At the pond in Herbert Park, my own father had lifted his trilby to the weather-blown poet Patrick Kavanagh, who wore no hat at all but went bravely bareheaded before both Creation and convention; and he took a kind of professional pride, my dad did, in the fact that Myles na gCopaleen had died in his care in a ward in Mercer's Hospital, a circumstance I would have thought of as something of a blot and a blunder in any self-respecting surgeon's curriculum vitae. But the reciprocal regard for scribes and for scripts was larger than local taste. The burning of books, the Nazi stormtroopers' Hallowe'en bonfire of modernist thinking which was also the *auto da fé* of the German intellect in the mid-Thirties of the last century, featured photographically in the History syllabus at school, though there was no accompanying picture of the cover of the Censorship of Publications Act by means of which the booted state authorities here stamped on any stray spark of imagination by our émigré artists.

More controversial at the time were the flimsy missalettes that had replaced prayer books in the reformed public worship of catholic Christianity. Traditionalists contended that these disposable flyers would diminish, and even neutralise, the magical dignity of scripture as the revealed Word of God in large, leather-bound volumes whose medicinal scent smelled a little like well-off ladies, while the innovators, who had fallen in love with cyclostyled sheets and seditious hand-outs in the rebellious run-up to 1968, dreamed of the Bible as a sum of blood-stained bulletins from the breeze blocks of a Latin American backdrop. In reality, both parties were repeating the polar terms of an earlier dispute, for, in the approach to the Russo-Japanese War of 1905, rabbis in the Pale of Settlement had permitted poor Jewish conscripts en route to their deaths in Manchuria to listen to a recorded form of the synagogue service on primitive Edison cylinders, the forgotten precursors of the acetate gramophone, provided that, in the immediate aftermath of this Sabbath worship, both the audio and its equipment were destroyed according to a prescribed ritual of immolation in order to protect the sanctity of God's discourse. Even now, in a post-religious society that has banalised almost every form of rapture in the human economy, from erection to Resurrection, that moment in the Mass when the president holds the gospel up high for the hosanna of the faithful in speech or in song embodies the power and prestige of writing as costly treasure, the signature of our species, down through the ages. In similar style, the creed incorporates that massive phrase 'according to the scriptures', 'kata tas graphas', as an act of homage to the miracle of the symbolic system we call writing, which is, all said and done, our grasp of time, our guardian angel, our genetic memory.

In light of these interminable preliminaries, what are we to make of today's reading from the book of Mark and of its very denigratory dismissal of scribes as such? Admittedly, its invective could be worse. In the preferred gospel of the Latin Church, Matthew's maledictions against them probably constitute incitement to hatred under the Act, while his pantomime horse, his two-headed monster, the conjoint scribes and Pharisees, frequently metamorphoses into a conspiracy theorist's culpable cultural triumvirate of priests, elders and scribes, a demonic ménage a trois to terrify the bejasus out of any God-fearing

Christian. Even in his mythical infancy narrative of the three oriental astronomers in search of the star-child, Matthew has presented the scribes as Herod's criminal creatures, the lickspittle apparatchiks of a paranoid Roman client, just as Mark mocks their pretensions to teaching authority at the outset of his shorter account.

Such polemical caricature passed for credible characterisation for almost two millennia before being interrogated, but propaganda of any kind can still tell us something substantial about its sources, at least about possible factors if not about probable facts. The unanimous defamation of the scribes in the three synoptic texts must reflect the actual antagonisms of early Christianity in its conflict with Judaism, and almost certainly reveals a concrete enmity towards them on the part of Jesus himself during his historic ministry in Galilee and Judea. He was, after all, both profoundly anti-clerical and anti-religious in regard to the institutional celebration of the Temple cult. On the other hand, as Meier remarks in the third volume of his marvellous work *A Marginal Jew*, the very ferocity of the Christian vendetta against the scribes serves paradoxically to authenticate the historicity of last Sunday's scripture in which Jesus and one laudable scribe shake hands rather than heads over the dual love of God and neighbour, since the oral tradition would have banished all mention of this embarrassing encounter with its displeasing pleasantness if it hadn't been widely witnessed and corroborated.

'Sofer' is the Hebrew noun for scribe, 'grammateus' the Greek equivalent, but the word in either language is really a serviceable shorthand for all manner of official and semi-official functionaries in court and chancery, from copyists to chroniclers to critics to commentators. A contemporary parallel, in terms of tactical impressiveness and strategic opacity, might be the term 'consultant,' that catch-all, carpet-bagging category of the Celtic Tiger. A fluid, fair-weather class within the religious intelligentsia, scribes enjoyed the exaggerated status of all scribblers in any illiterate culture and were, I imagine, correspondingly protectionist about their skills in the interest of their salaries. But their talents and training were essential to the careful transmission of the Judeo-Christian texts that constitute Western culture, and Jesus' resentment of the guild may have stemmed in part from his being snubbed by them as a country bumpkin. The best and brightest in their ranks modelled their learned ministry on the great prototypes of the Hebrew scriptures, from the post-exilic Ezra to the long-suffering Eleazar of the Maccabean wars, and they located the terms of their trade in the splendid, if slightly snobbish, resumé provided in the thirty-ninth chapter of the Book of Ecclesiasticus where the job description states that:

> the wisdom of a scribe cometh by his time of leisure: and he that is less in action, shall receive wisdom. He shall seek out the wisdom of all the ancients, and will be occupied in the prophets. He will seek out the sayings of renowned men, and will enter withal into the subtleties of parables. He will search out the hidden meanings of proverbs, and will be conversant in the secrets of parables. He will give his heart to resort early to the Lord that made him, and he will pray in the sight of the Most High. He will open his mouth in prayer, and make supplication for his sins. For if it shall please the great Lord, he will fill him with the spirit of understanding.

This isn't a despicable spec, as specs go. Parasites and impersonators may be the partial verdict of an excluded outsider, a culchie come to town and sneered at by the varsity sorts. Yet the Lord's dismissal of their camp and frippery does hit home, if only because of a certain autobiographical anxiety. I am myself, after all, a scribe of sorts, one who presumes to gossip about very grave matters from the shelter of a sterile studio in a centrally-heated catacomb in Donnybrook, Dublin 4; and I am therefore prey to the same performative guile and grandstanding as the clerics Jesus ridicules. Not only am I prey but predator too, for, while I have always wanted to be a fool rather than a knave, there is nothing to prevent one from being both at the same time, especially in matters of faith and quarrels.

Secular emails from a Jewish friend of mine always begin in the top-right corner with the letters BH, the abbreviated form of *Baruch Hashem*, Glory to the Lord. Perhaps I should copy that ancient scribal usage, revert to the childhood style of any student taught by the Js in Ireland, and write out the wobbly capitals AMDG in blue ballpoint at the top of every homework exercise in my grubby copybooks. *Ad Maiorem Dei Gloriam*: To the Greater Glory of God. The logo is no guarantee of goodness, academic or ethical, but it somehow consecrates even soiled and spoiled attempts at meaning to the greater glory of God. Wasn't it Chesterton who said that a thing worth doing was worth doing badly? The alternative is to run the risk of Wittgenstein's terrible jibe; for, as that saintly mystic strode from the high table in Trinity Hall, Cambridge, he remarked to the repatriated (and rather hungry) ex-prisoner Ian Watt, 'I have lost my appetite. The conversation is neither from the heart nor from the head.'

Chapter Thirty-One
MORE REVELATIONS

IN THE ABSENCE or abduction of my beloved Authorised Version, a dishevelled copy of which ought to be somewhere or other in the warm landslide underneath my office desk, I'm having to google a quote in the New American Bible edition from today's gospel reading, a choice incidentally which omits much more interesting ambient material from the same admonitory discourse. Under the sign of strict secrecy, the Lord confides to his very favourite followers, Peter, James and John (for even Jesus had his A list) that 'in those days after that tribulation the sun will be darkened, and the moon will not give its light, and the stars will be falling from the sky, and the powers in the heavens will be shaken.' All of this, we discover by reading the aptly captioned Chapter 13 in the earliest life of Christ, is only for starters, a catastrophic cosmic chorus line behind a still more dreadful spotlight on the sight of human society sinking psychotically into what the thermonuclear choreographers in Washington and Moscow used to call Mutual Assured Destruction, or MAD for short.

If this is what the scholars call the 'little apocalypse' in Saint Mark (13), we should perhaps pray to be preserved from the larger variety; but our petition won't be answered, or, better, it was answered long ago in the eastern Mediterranean by the clerical compilers of the canon of sacred writings. Despite resistance and refusal by some Christian communities in the world of late antiquity, the Book of Revelation was eventually installed in the scriptural quantum of the New Testament. Worse again, it was given a privileged position at the end of the collection, signifying not only the close of composition but the disclosure of the eschatological endtime, the Omega point, the hour zero, in an orgy of fierce, bifocal judgement, of thunderous reward and reprisal, that appears to annihilate the historical Jesus' authentic agenda of non-violent reconciliation between the children of the one Father.

Some of its lingo, even the more lurid detail, may have occurred as symbolic, semitic speech in his teaching and preaching, but it did not originate in him. Apocalyptic thinking was popular and even populist in the several Judaisms of his time, just as it is in our own destabilised, post-religious occident, in which the vengefulness of Armageddon provides a congenial, customised scenario for the private or the political rehearsal of our personal resentments. Down in the saline stench of the Dead Sea in the Qumran commune, the ascetical Essene fanatics aspired in Jesus' own era to the purged kingdom of the elect who alone would receive the benediction of a Moloch they mistook for a Messiah. Similarly, in the first letter to the Thessalonians, which is the oldest document in the Christian literary deposit, that astounding compound figure, Paul the Apostle–Saul the Pharisee, sketches an eschatological exit from history which Mark himself may have drawn upon a generation later as he assembled his stark narrative. In parallel with the prophetic idiom, a whole transcultural train of false prophets, from Plato to Pol Pot, from Robespierre to the racial lawyers of the Reich, have tried to diversify this sterile endeavour at the singular instead of the plural, and their only harvest has ever been hecatombs of merely human cadavers.

That, of course, is the opposite of Jesus' proclamation since he had invariably celebrated the reprobate as the righteous of God. But he had undoubtedly inhaled the terror and theatricality of eschatological images from infancy. Just as he would individualise the national emblem of the suffering servant in second Isaiah, so too he adopted from the verses of the Book of Daniel the mysterious motif of the archangelic 'son of man' which, whether we agree with the great exegete Geza Vermes that the term really amounts to saying 'one' or 'myself' rather than 'I' in self-reference or whether we accept it as a major messianic self-appellation, was certainly Jesus' own chosen usage. Did he in reality anticipate a cataclysm? Very possibly. Did he exalt it? Not at all. Without the benefit of Trinitarian theology and the commentaries of the Cappadocian Fathers which would require the slow passage of chronological centuries, the real-life Jesus lacked divine foreknowledge of such phenomena to an extent that embarrassed his near and later contemporaries. If apocalyptic expectation had been part of his imaginative placenta as a representative Jew, it was regarded as shrivelled afterbirth by the early Church which was more concerned to domesticate and eventually to internalise the notion of the Kingdom of God, converting it from fire to water, from air to earth, and from the shock of drastic imminence into the task of tranquil immanence. As Hans Kung reminds us in his lovely elucidation of the faith in his Credo, the two angels in the opening section of Saint Luke's Acts of the Apostles speak in a single voice when they rebuke the dreamy retinue of Jesus by saying to them, 'You men of Galilee, why do you stand staring up into heaven?' It is a sensible summons to this sphere and not to any other, to the tedious, terrestrial order; for, as the French poet Philippe Jacottet has said; 'There is another world, and it is this one.'

To be sure, the three traditions of Abraham have each sanctified radiant, if not radioactive, apocalypses (though it was at least mischievous of the Jewish physicist Robert Oppenheimer to call his atomic holocaust at Los Alamos in July 1945 by the Christian term 'Trinity'). The Koranic proclivity to inflict upon its faithful a most anthropomorphic vision of the justice of

Judgement on the last day is well matched in the brimstone bulletins of ancestral Christianity, both verbal and visual, polemic and fresco, which culminated, when the four Beatles were babies, in the only verifiable Jewish plot at all, a large part of Poland where innocent millions drifted down as soot and ashes in the war years; while the radical renewal of the face of the earth in biblical Judaism itself found its distorted twentieth century form in the breeze block inferno of Marxist communism. Not that I'm sneering at any of these perversions from a higher vantage. The neo-liberal line in eschatology, a free market, free-for-all future of one man, one house and garden with garage, promises eco-death, the planet as property – a limitless planetary suburb, in fact, if one remembers that 'suburb' is the Latin for the little white streets of a cemetery.

From inkhorn to hard copy and from letterpress to laptops, two centuries of historical-critical scholarship haven't settled the crunch question: Was the Gospel of Mark written immediately before or immediately after the destruction of the Temple in Jerusalem by the hard-bitten troops of Titus in the year 69 of the common calendar? If it was written before the sack of the sanctuary, was Jesus' actual philistine indifference to the majesty of its monumental masonry capable of being construed by later Christians as divine prevision of its pillage? If it was written after the eradication of the Jewish theocracy and the dispersal of its people by the Roman army, did the gospel craftily reconfigure the recent past, retrospectively ascribing to the crucified rabbi powers of prophecy he didn't possess?

But the timetabling of the truth-telling is, it seems to me, neither here nor there. A cursory look at the little apocalypse infers what close reading only verifies. All the calamities that the Lord catalogues as he sits there upon the Mount of Olives 'over against the Temple' (for, you see, I've found my Authorised Version again under an old copy of *The Irish Catholic* and an empty vinyl sleeve for the LP 'Picnic at Hanging Rock'), all those calamities, I say, are commonplace. Wars, rumours of wars, nation against nation, famine, troubles, terror, court cases, condemnation, punishment, peril and pandemonium – this is the stuff of the working week, the daily tabloids of the Law, the broken and embittered world we embody, each of us, all of us, all the time, from presidents to prisoners, from parliamentarians to paramilitaries, from the able-bodied to the disabled. Nothing human is alien to any of us, as the playwright Terence wrote two thousand years ago, and the whole parterre of the amphitheatre rose up in recognition at the time to render that sentence ovation after ovation, because it isn't a vindictive dictum but an optimistic outcry. In Luther's famous formula of the mystical enmeshment of the ordained and the ordinary, if the apocalypse were to happen at daybreak, we should still get up with the sun to plant our apple tree; just as Kennedy's ultimatum to Khrushchev in the rigid reciprocal conflict of the superpowers over Soviet missiles in Cuba and American missiles in Turkey did not prevent those foolish fond old men, the bishops and archbishops in their bonnets, from walking on the very same day in 1962 into the Sistine Chapel to start the Second Vatican Council, which was, if one separates the baloney from the bones of it, a heartfelt, heartbreaking effort to explore the paths of peace like the Palestinian founder.

I thought of that, the pontiff and the Pentagon and the failed house party my parents had given on that sombre October evening in the early 60s, when I went North to Belfast as an undergraduate to listen to a lecture thirty years ago at a time of bin lids clattering warnings in the back streets and the rotor hum of helicopter blades above the roof slates. I was lodged in a room left vacant by a girl who had gone away for the weekend. Under the drab slant of the ceiling over the angle poise, and across from the fluffy quilt on her high-flown bed, she had pinned a laminate wall chart of the year and its divisions. With a permanent fluorescent pen she had marked in messages, birthdays, tutorials, dinners, a hospital appointment, a hair appointment; and, in among these quick cursive characters in bright black and blue, the jittery shorthand of time, she had drawn deliberately on each twenty-eighth day in Day-Glo violet a beautiful shining stencil of the letter P, like the illuminated capital in the calf-skin pages of a Celtic psalter.

Hope for the future, faith in the present, charity toward the past. There was no fear for the world on her watch, whatever the wind did to her damp dormer window. She knew intuitively, it seems to me, what the young theologian James Alison has expressed so exquisitely in his early work *Raising Abel*: that the apocalypse arrived long since, that the master of the house has indeed already come; that he came at evening in the Last Supper, at midnight in the garden, at cockcrow in the tears of Peter, and in the morning in the rubbish dump of Skull Place. And we are in a state of wonder. We are wide awake.

Chapter Thirty-Two
MINDING GOD

LONG, LONG AGO, I was living happily ever after here in the coal smoke and diesel fumes of Dublin town, teaching a Confirmation class in Belvedere College in the final, flickering months of the somewhat concussed pontificate of Pope Paul VI, an aristocratic Bishop of Rome who was known, I'm told, to his own civil service in the Vatican as Papa Amletico, Pope Hamlet, the prevaricating vicar of Christ. Each morning I'd arrive in the classroom to coach the kids – a case, I'm afraid, of the bland leading the bland, because, at twenty-one years of age, I was, of course, far too old for religion and far too young for faith – and we'd chat together, in the companionable, manly scent of thirty little fellows, myself included, who'd cycled strenuously from far and wide through centre-city traffic and who were now drying their footwear on the hot radiator, about the meaning of mystery and the mystery of meaning. God forgive me is all I can say. I even remember one time asking them what the odour of sanctity meant (and you may well want to know in return why on earth I was talking such drivel to twelve-year-olds in 1977), and a rather grubby angel at the back – bunny teeth, retainer, lovely lank hair over a high forehead – put up his blackened hand to say that it was when you stank to high heaven.

Believe it or not, the same scamp had a crush on me, and I was as shy as a débutante about it. Being the last in a long family, I had never had the opportunity to be idolised by a younger brother, and this pupil's devotion – he would carry my briefcase for me to the bus stop on O'Connell Street after school – charmed, disarmed and alarmed me. After all, I had to be worthy of his worship. I couldn't even smoke until he waved me off. For the first time in my life, I saw things from my heterosexual sister's point of view. You have to be on your toes, if not in your high heels, when a suitor calls. But I was still a bit broken-hearted when, at the start of the new school year, the same student met me with complete indifference. None of the priests in the community house had told me in advance about the psychological spurts of growth that occur during the summer holidays between the junior and the senior house. They let me find out the hard way.

My beautiful boy admirer, who is now probably a destitute solicitor or a bankrupt obstetrician, gave me yet another gift, equally enduring, in the form of a weekend essay in a copy book, five hundred blue ballpoint words on being Robinson Crusoe – I recall the colour because the pages photocopied badly, as blue ink, for reasons beyond me, always will. Now I was obviously spending more time at the time in the snug of Doheny Nesbitt's than in the quiet carrels of a library in Trinity, because anyone who's ever taught children will tell you that the desert island topic is only one merit bar above the redundant 'A Day in the Life of a Penny Coin'. Even so, I got some grand submissions – for that's what an essay means, an attempt, a try-out – full of parrots and pirates and, in the case of the couple of kids who'd already hit puberty and whose cheeks, as Pindar says somewhere, in an Olympian ode, 'were darkening with down', some congenial castaway women as well to perpetuate the buccaneers. But most of the stories were littered in a lively, partly legible way with 'I did this' and 'I did that' and 'I did the other', much indeed like the original seventeenth century novel by Daniel Defoe (by the way, Foe added the 'de' to make his name nobler), the chapter headings of which very economic fiction mainly begin with that same disingenuous capital letter, the upright I which doubles, to the detriment of anyone speaking and thinking in English, as the mathematical Number One: moi, me, my own free-standing self, that titular, titanic entity we're all supposed, in today's idiom, to take absolute ownership of, as the precondition of personal happiness.

What made my cherub's composition interesting was something else altogether. Like every other classmate, he had been shipwrecked in the first paragraph; but he hadn't killed or enslaved the natives in the second, nor had he discovered oil, diamonds and uranium (or blondes in bikinis) in the third. Instead, from the sunken debris of his shattered vessel he had conserved sufficient timber and ball-bearings to construct the carriage of a gigantic telescope. From the fine sand on the seashore he had chosen the purest particles only, and become in good order and in gradual stages over a whole decade a glass-blower, shaping from his own breath and burnt lips a series of long-distance lenses that allowed him, for the second ten years of his prosperous solitude, to scan the firmament and the face of the Deep. Remote galaxies floated like agile bacteria into his sights, white dwarves and red giants, dark matter and bright matter, the gravity of God's imploded universe, a glowing cat-scan of the Body of Christ in the glorious cosmos. A scientist in saffron, this Crusoe was at peace in his paradise.

Came a stiff breeze, a sea swell, a storm cloud, and, finally, a Shakespearian Tempest, and his telescope was toppled. It lay around him in scintillating smithereens. He grieved keenly and cleanly, for the grief of bereavement is love without any pretension, a lethal, live-giving thing. Then he set to work without any vengeance at all. From the infinitesimal ruins of his astronomer's looking glass, splinters and ball-bearing chips, he constructed in subliminal minuteness the trillion bits of an anatomist's tiny electron microscope. It took him ten years in all, but, for a further ten after that, he enticed the underworld itself into his electrostatic field of vision – into those very 'visions during the night' of which today's first reading from the Book of Daniel speaks. Agile bacteria floated like remote galaxies into his sights, red giants and white dwarves, the venous and arterial systems of dustmites he had shaken from his eyebrows as specimens, the gravity of God's exploded universe, an ultrascan of the infant and the infinite infrared realm. All in all, he had been forty years in his desert island, and the time had passed in the twinkling of his two eyes.

At this point in the parable, a boat arrived suddenly out of nowhere and brought him back to Dún Laoghaire. I imagine his mother, a person from Porlock, had told him it was too late to be doing homework on a Sunday evening and he should go to bed at once. But the little scholar had already proved himself to be a sage as well. If a philosopher were to define the worth of his wisdom, he/she might say that a youngster had shown the way from the Promethean to the Epimethean world. In so doing, he had demonstrated the prayerfulness which enables us not only to survive disaster but to endure it. In this ember month, this Mí na Marbh, this last solemn Sunday in Ordinary Time, in the slow and sombre approach to the patience of the fast of Advent, we who have lost our telescope, our map of the heavens, could do worse than copy the holy doggedness of my Man Friday friend. For only detail can save us now.

Poet Dennis O'Driscoll in a marvellous poem called 'Missing God' offers just such sustaining detail in a litany, a November altar list of the dead which includes the dying of the altars themselves. So, since I've plagiarised a school essay from the 70s of the late last century, let me steal as well a senior writer's service of vespers for the millennium.

Missing God

His grace is no longer called for
before meals: farmed fish multiply
without His intercession.
Bread production rises through
disease-resistant grains devised
scientifically to mitigate His faults.

Yet, though we rebelled against Him
like adolescents, uplifted to see
an oppressive father banished –
a bearded hermit – to the desert,
we confess to missing Him at times.

Miss Him during the civil wedding
when, at the blossomy altar
of the registrar's desk, we wait in vain
to be fed a line containing words
like 'everlasting' and 'divine'.

Miss Him when the TV scientist
explains the cosmos through equations,
leaving our planet to revolve on its axis
aimlessly, a wheel skidding in snow.

Miss Him when the radio catches a snatch
of plainchant from some echoey priory;
when the gospel choir raises its collective voice
to ask *Shall We Gather at the River?*
or the forces of the oratorio converge
on *I Know That My Redeemer Liveth*
and our contracted hearts lose a beat.

Miss Him when a choked voice at
the crematorium recites the poem
about fearing no more the heat of the sun.

Miss Him when we stand in judgement
on a lank Crucifixion in an art museum,
its stripe-like ribs testifying to rank.

Miss Him when the gamma-rays
recorded on the satellite graph
seem arranged into a celestial score,
the music of the spheres,
the *Ave Verum Corpus* of the observatory lab.

Miss Him when we stumble on the breast lump
for the first time and an involuntary prayer
escapes our lips; when a shadow crosses
our bodies on an x-ray screen; when we receive
a transfusion of foaming blood
sacrificed anonymously to save life.

Miss Him when we exclaim His name
spontaneously in awe and anger
as a woman in a birth ward
calls to her long-dead mother.

Miss Him when the linen-covered
dining table holds warm bread rolls,
shiny glasses of red wine.

Miss Him when a dove swoops
from the orange grove in a tourist village
just as the monastery bell begins to take its toll.

Miss Him when our journey leads us
under leaves of Gothic tracery, an arch
of overlapping branches that meet
like hands in Michelangelo's *Creation*.

Miss Him when, trudging past a church,
we catch a residual blast of incense,
a perfume on par with the fresh-baked loaf
which Milosz compared to happiness.

Miss Him when our newly-fitted kitchen
comes in Shaker-style and we order
a matching set of Mother Anne Lee chairs.

Miss Him when we listen to the prophecy
of astronomers that the visible galaxies
will recede as the universe expands.

Miss Him when the sunset makes
its presence felt in the stained glass
window of the fake antique lounge bar.

Miss Him the way an uncoupled glider
riding the evening thermals misses its tug.

Miss Him, as the lovers shrugging
shoulders outside the cheap hotel
ponder what their next move should be.

Even feel nostalgic, odd days,
for His Second Coming,
like standing in the brick
dome of a dovecote
after the birds have flown.

Chapter Thirty-Three
NEITHER KING NOR KAISER

A MATE OF MINE joshed me during the week for having ignored last Sunday's celebration of the feast of Christ the King, which is, after all, the high, heraldic finale of the Roman Catholic Church year. Was I, he wondered, a residual republican, incapable of congratulating retired monarchal metaphors in a meritocratic culture? Actually, I'm as crypto-royalist as the next Irishman, a proclivity we proved beyond reasonable doubt a quarter of a century ago when an assault on the British embassy in Ballsbridge was followed a fortnight later by the whole nation taking the day off work to watch the late Diana Spencer marry Charles Windsor in Saint Paul's Cathedral. But my friend had indeed touched a tender spot, if not a theological tabu. Christians of the Western Patriarchate, as the Eastern tradition calls us erring RCs, are not at home in the browbeating Byzantine mode where the stern and sovereign Lord glares down from a glittering gold dome or icon at his muddy subjects. The look of him can seem more hostile than hospitable to humdrum European parishioners who were raised on first-name terms with Jesus of Nazareth rather than in formal fashion with Christ the Pantocrator, the Caliph of the cosmos. That balance between humanity and divinity, between Son of Man and Son of God, between carpenter and creator, halo and cradle-cap, has always been and will always remain the particular and impossible duty of the Latin-rite remnant for whom, unlike so many majestic dissenters of either exclusive emphasis, a greasy foetus in the blood of afterbirth can be God's word to the world.

To be sure, Pope Pius XI, the absolute ruler who instituted the Mass of Christ the King in 1925, was thinking in terms of a more regal arrival than a brat with whooping cough in a lean-to full of livestock. But it must have seemed a truly eccentric title for the Pontiff to have selected at a time when thrones had toppled worldwide and precarious apprentice democracies were making firewood of such furniture. The war of the three cousins had ended less than a decade before, an entire continental generation of conscript teenage males was slowly manuring much of the arable land from the river Marne to the city of Minsk, and, in the catastrophe that had overtaken an Emperor, a Tsar and a Kaiser, dynastic chit-chat struck the secular ear as irrelevant and even irreverent. Moreover, the biblical academics who had somehow survived the papal pogroms of the anti-modernist era at the start of the century had by this stage established credibly that, from a traditional Judaic perspective, Jesus was not an eligible Davidic candidate for any kind of kingship and that the proof texts his disciples adduced in the Hebrew scriptures were, in many respects, the opportunistic readings of a tiny minority against the reasonable rabbinic consensus. The blue-blooded pedigrees provided for the Lord by two of the evangelists, Matthew and Luke, constitute complex theological legends and not genealogical data. Indeed, the very idea of a Galilean messiah is a paradox amounting to an oxymoron, a contradiction in terms.

Whether the Holy Father was thinking dialectically is difficult to determine. Perhaps he was pining, post Garibaldi and pre-Concordat, for the restoration of his temporal authority in the former papal territories where his immediate nineteenth century predecessors had kept their court, their consiglieres, and, for that matter, their hereditary executioner as well. For the statehood of the Lateran does perpetuate, in a manner so modest as to be miniature, the ethos of the enormous fantasy that underlay the founding of Constantinople, the decree of Constantine, the cult of Charlemagne, and a thousand other associated megalomaniacal delusions since then: that the law of love may become the law of the land by edict, that ethics may be enforceable by persuasion of power alone, that Christianity itself may eventuate in Christendom, that Christendom may thereby reinforce the writ and remit of scriptural imperatives, and that the Kingdom of God, despite its own noisy protestations to the contrary in every page of the New Testament, may yet prove to be of this world after all. Satan, be it said, made the very same offer to Jesus as his third and terminal temptation during the Lord's sabbatical in the desert; and it is precisely Christ's threefold refusal of power, prestige and possessiveness that constitutes the sinlessness that has always been ascribed to him by his flawed and fascinated entourage. For if he is a monarch, it is only in a topsy-turvy, Twelfth Night fashion, his crown of coronation a tiara of briars, his seat of enthronement the electric chair, and his purple imperial apparel the parodistic sackcloth of a jester, like the ridiculed cap-and-bells clown of George Rouault's engravings. In fact, we cannot truly intuit Christ unless we first identify him as the authentic anti-Christ, the opponent of all anointed echelons, the reversal and inversion of the type of the tyrant, the indefatigable disappointment, in short, of all our secular and sacred expectations of him.

This is obviously a problem for us. Our second nature – if it's not indeed primary – is to defer, revere and venerate, or, in the photographic negative of the same need, to resent and resist. Schoolchildren will always and everywhere know the names of the kids in the higher classes, not in the lower. Those below us are by the same token beneath us. Hierarchies obsess us; hegemonies engross us. Snakes and ladders is the board game of choice. 'The bigs hit me and so I hit the smalls,' said a middle-sized pupil to Bertrand Russell when he was training as a teacher; and, to the end of his long, non-violent life, that very English philosopher regarded the moderate boy's outburst as the best epitome of the human endeavour he had ever encountered. In this somewhat subdued understanding of the social enterprise, a king emerges only as bully number one in the heavyweight heave-ho of things, a pyramidal point on a slave-labour building site. And yet it's possible that poor Pius XI, so far from being anachronistic, was ahead of his time. The second half of his pontificate coincided with the consolidation of the Fascist states in Europe. Persisting German Christians, in particular, now prayed the Lord's Prayer –

> Unser Vater im Himmel,
> dein Name werde geheiligt,
> dein Reich komme –

with a renewed and a radicalised sense of its utter antipathy to the pseudo-kingdom of Hitler's state, the self-styled thousand-year Reich, 'des tausendjahrigen Reiches', an ancient synonym for the millennium that profiteered parasitically under the Nazis from its previous medieval Christian and utopian resonances. A similar irony might well have informed the Hellenistic first-century followers of the crucified convict, since, according to several contemporary scholars, the Greek noun 'Basileia' which we commonly translate from the gospels as 'kingdom' would be much better rendered as 'empire' in recognition that the word was employed by early Christian communities in an act of deliberate sabotage of the term 'imperium', the substantive that officially denoted the global Roman culture of coercion and conquest, the swastika and jackboot of its day. So the empire of God which Jesus proclaims is the perfect paradoxical antithesis of statecraft and dominion, and will in its turn be proclaimed, in the latter, legal sense of being outlawed, by the star chambers of the status quo. Historian and homilist Eamon Duffy reminds us how perilous that Christian irony was, for the persecuting emperor Domitian, who had been divinised by his more discerning apparatchiks in the Senate, described himself as Kyrios or Lord, and the day devoted to the praise of his apotheosis, with all its obligatory rubrics, was saluted accordingly as the Lord's Day.

Last week's commemoration of the kingship of Christ and of his sardonic subversion of imperial nomenclature may, accordingly, be as useful an introduction to the season of Advent as today's choice of texts in the lectionary. It may even be more *ad rem* insofar as it presents the crowning scriptural theme of the victim as victor, the beggar as regent, an unearthly exaltation of the downtrodden, and, above all else, the extraordinary pantomime of the paschal mystery in which merely human values, fixated as they are on the fetishes of executive authority, are deconstructed in fierce, forensic detail by the egalitarian gaze of God. After all, the prescribed reading from Jeremiah, which doesn't occur in the Septuagint, is not in fact by Jeremiah but by a much later student of his tradition and idiom, while the Pauline letter to the Thessalonians is signed by an apostle who was notoriously indifferent to the public ministry, let alone the private nativity, of the crucified and risen Christ. Even the gospel lection is only the Lucan version of the terrible thirteenth chapter in Mark that was preached a fortnight ago. Perhaps a monarch in motley, the chequered Christ as a parti-coloured harlequin, is a better guide to the baby wrapped in bandages like a barber's pole in a galvanised silo in Bethlehem.

In this time of waiting, this task of attentiveness, this night watch through the small hours that is the whole travail of Advent, we are not called to be bleakly sceptical about the business of being human, beset as it is by the abominable phantoms of caste and class, but to be comically counter-intuitive in the manner of our Maker whose wise mischief can never deceive. It would be easy to despond, for, of all things, the passage of time does not occur like clockwork, and the solstice remains the winter's darkest secret. The restless trees are losing their hair like cancer victims as we sit hunched over low fires, logs soaked in paraffin, watching on our plasma television sets atrocities interspersed with Christmas advertisements. There will be no room at the inn because of the office parties. Yet that 'roaring of the waters', that 'échousés thalassés' that the Lord speaks of in today's gospel rehabilitates the primal meaning of the bitter baptismal element in which we must sink and swim to become the light-hearted of the kingdom of laughter. We are asked to be out of our depth, summoned to a burial at sea. It is not a Kodak moment, this, but a crisis, not a genteel spattering of pre-heated droplets on a sedated infant but a deep sea change in the salt and darkness of adult drowning. So we are neither pessimists nor Polyannas, but unsure shore liners, beachcombers on the brink of vision. Beyond the escritoire of the legate Quirinius and his Italian secretaries, beyond the poll tax predictions of local tallymen, beyond all calculation and census taking, we await the utter illiteracy of the wordless word.

Chapter Thirty-Four
CHRISTENING
THE BAPTIST

BAGHDAD, BABYLON, BABEL. It was during a previous conflict in the same stricken strategic region of the Middle East, that of the atrocious carnage of the Iran-Iraq war in the 1980s which the American Secretary of Defence Caspar Weinberger notoriously rubbished at the time as a battle between 'two four-letter countries', that I first heard of the little communities called Mandaeans who live, or at any rate persist precariously, in parts of Mesopotamia that were marked on my school atlas not as a nation state or as an Ottoman province but as British Petroleum, Royal Dutch Shell and Standard Oil; and I sometimes wonder still, a quarter century later, whether these gentle folk are enduring the present symmetrical sectarian horrors in their occupied homeland or emigrating at extortionate expense like their more orthodox Christian cousins towards the less sadistic possibilities of a future elsewhere. 'Cousins' I call them instead of brothers or brethren because, while they have a Christ whom they proclaim, an anointed whom they exalt, he is not Jesus of Nazareth but the somewhat sterner first century contemporary whom the Christian scriptures represent for emblematic purposes as a close blood relative of the Redeemer: and that is John the Baptist.

Perhaps I've already revealed the bias intrinsic to my own Christian beliefs by describing this parallel Messiah of the Mandaean congregation as stern. Locusts and honey is, admittedly, a less sociable diet than bread and wine, although, in the last paragraphs of the Gospel of Saint John, Our Lord sits down to savour a dripping honeycomb along with a fillet of fresh fish. This may be a menu by association since Jesus, rather surprisingly, is about to reprise the Baptist's basic manifesto, namely the preaching of repentance for the remission of sins among all nations, beginning at Jerusalem; but it serves, in every sense, to underscore a motif of continuity between the two individuals, when discontinuity, a rift amounting to a rupture, a counterpoint verging on contrast, tends to be the preferred emphasis both in traditional devotion and in theological doctrine.

Indeed, there are times when the Christian stress on the sternness and austerity of John the Baptist disguises a discreet anti-semitism, as much to say, since the poor prophetic man is supposed to embody the pilgrim and the path-finding Hebrew people, that the Old Testament is gloomy while the New Testament is glad. It may arguably be the case that John in the desert mandates repentance as the road to forgiveness while Jesus in the tavern blithely reverses those terms and conditions, offering forgiveness first and foremost as the flourishing route to a fresh start afterwards; but it would be wrong to picture the precursor of the Lord as dark and dehydrated, a masculine ascetic stinking of a goat-skin girdle as he staggers about in sunstroke and a stream of moral consciousness. In fact, he may be claimed correctly as a feminist prototype as well as a Hermes figure, since it is he who universalises the hitherto private female ritual of sacral washing after the rigours of menstruation. From that secret, sidelined culture of marginal women in a male order, the Baptist brings forth a new protocol to purify the heart, to enlarge and emancipate renewed, replenished, revitalised life. Henceforth, total immersion in the warm uterine waters of the world will re-energise depleted persons who thirst from the depths of their own human particularity for the depths of their own human profundity, the Deep that is within them, the Red

Sea of their selves parting like the bursting liquids of the labour of birthing.

No wonder then, to the horror of his later household, that Jesus joined John's open-air college, studied at his school, wandered with him in the wilderness, sought and received the master's blessing, bowed down for baptism, was born again and braced for mission. He may even have learned from his startling tutor the leniencies of feminine thinking that would mark his ministry to the glorious beginning of its ghastly end. Mark in his account of Jesus' journey is surely right to insist on his historical apprenticeship to the Baptist as a real *fons et origo*, an actual fountainhead, 'arché tou evaggeliou', the start of the great good news.

The other evangelists, be it said, find this probationary perspective disagreeable. Matthew is quick to incorporate a significantly softening tradition within the high talk of his community that remembered instead a mortified Baptist refusing Jesus' request to be baptised by him in the blue-green Jordan currents. Luke, in his turn, situates the event of the meeting at the river most scrupulously in the political and sacerdotal chronology of the day, listing innumerable unpronounceable dignitaries of council chamber and chapel, from Tiberius to the tetrarchs and the Temple pontiffs, yet he slides discreetly and disingenuously over John's participation as Jesus' senior in the administration of the sacrament. By the time Saint John presents his portrayal of the commission of Jesus by John at the end of the first century, the Lord doesn't enter or exit from the water at all while the Baptist emerges from his watering down not as a powerful executor but as a privileged eyewitness to the enfleshed Word of God.

Even in the radiant and incantatory prayerfulness of the prologue to his gospel, where transcendence of some incommensurable kind trembles in every syllable of its opening eighteen verses, John the Evangelist is still concerned at every opportunity to knock John the Baptist down to size. We may rationally infer what that reasonably implies: that rivalry and resentment continued throughout much of the first century between the messianic faction of Jesus on the one side and the messianic faction of John on the other, exacerbated by the clear consciousness on both banks, to the triumphalism of the older and the embarrassment of the younger group, that the Lord was indeed trained initially by his decapitated mentor. The gospels are replete with the reverberations of this stand-off between the two sects, and the after-echo can be overheard in Luke's second instalment of his writings, in the Book of Acts, where the Baptist's entourage interrogates the apostolic proselytizers of Jesus at Ephesus. Precedence and primacy are, after all, as basic as bread. In the end, whether the advocacy is synoptic or Johannine, the texts combine to accomplish a consensus which, when the canon of Christian scripture is finally consolidated, will reduce the irritating adversary to a herald and a harbinger and so eventually, in our own murderous millennium, to an antiquarian curiosity in southern Iraq and south-western Iran.

It may seem shabby to speak of complex theological testimony in this feet-of-clay fashion. John the Baptist has, of course, a strong typological function within the narratives that name him, but to insist upon the pettiness and the pathos of fact does not prevent its transfiguration into truth by the attention of love. The dove that hovers over Jesus' head as he surfaces in the stream after his baptism may have flown a great distance from its homely, humble roost in ancient eastern mythologies as the cute carrier pigeon of the Goddess of Love, but its flight path over the Jordan – a name that, as Saint Origen reminds us, means a descending, a coming down – is the wing-and-a-prayer of metaphor itself that guides us by grounding us in the density of the three-dimensional mundane. From an incarnational point of view, from the very perspective of the mystery of the Incarnation that the fourth gospel glosses, the Jesus of history must be the beating heart and the bloodstream of the Christ of faith.

As Karl Rahner declares in his *Foundations of Christian Faith*, 'the basic and decisive point of departure lies in an encounter with the historical Jesus of Nazareth, and hence in an ascending Christology'. There is no enmity between the two approaches, however much the polarised devotees of either avenue effervesce on the issue, and the evangelical record which reports both the history and the hermeneutic is similarly flawed and faithful. Augustine of Hippo, in a reflection repeated by Karl Barth in 1926 to a university audience in Munster that included uniformed Brownshirts among the believers in the terraces of the lecture theatre, understood this better than any when he wrote: 'Perhaps not even John the Evangelist himself has said it as it is, but only as he could, for a man has here spoken about God, a man enlightened by God, but still a man. Because he is enlightened, he has said something; if he had not been enlightened, he could have said nothing; but because he is an enlightened man, he has not said it all as it is, but only said it as a man can say it.'

From Marcion in the second century to Harnack in the twentieth, many students and scholars have sought to wrest the New Testament writings from their living roots in the salvation history of the Hebrew Bible. The thematic treatment of John the Baptist in the gospels utterly refutes such an attempt at truncation, since his profile in their pages recapitulates the advent stance of a whole people's prophetic watch through the persecuting ages. Indeed, the Baptist has pride of place as the first in a queue of annihilated witnesses which links him to Jesus and to Stephen and thence to Peter and Paul in a martyric procession of innocent casualties for the kingdom; for Herod will placate his retinue by slaughtering John just as Pontius Pilate will appease the populace by delivering the Lord to them. 'We tend to think,' argues Girardean exegete Gil Bailie, 'that the prophet gets rejected because of his message ... but it's also true that he has a message because he's been rejected.' In either case, John's eager and eschatological tidings – his contempt of pedigree, his critique of the concept of a chosen clientele, and his commitment to social justice as the true service of Yahweh – make him a candidate for the cleaver at any moment in any self-respecting religious culture. Hermit he may have been, but he was in no way hermetic. If the line in Luke is accurate, he even befriended the publicans before his pupil did.

At the end of his hectic schedule of chivalric sorties in the novel of his name, Cervantes' Don Quixote acknowledges on his deathbed that he's been bedevilled all his life by the cultural curriculum of compare and contrast. But this is more than Spanish say-so. If the relationship between John and Jesus had been written by a Greek, let's imagine, it would probably have resulted in the same old story of Agamemnon and Achilles as the Iliad recites it. Those two quivering competitors engage in a prestige struggle, founded on reciprocal fascination, in which mutual detestation masks their identical likeness, just as a cartoon dust-cloud features fists and feet but no faces. In Homer's poem, their selfish squabble will help to sink a whole Hellenic civilisation irretrievably. They are, in fact, the major-domos of absolute mayhem in the eastern Mediterranean. In John's Judaic context, however, there is imitation without conflict, attraction without antagonism, relationship without rivalry. There is even, perish the thought, the subversive suggestion that harmony may arise from hierarchy, and that subordination may be a supreme state. 'He must increase and I must decrease.' What a motto for our managerial world.

Chapter Thirty-Five
GAUDETE!

YESTERDAY'S SUNSET in the lenient, later afternoon of the third Sunday in Advent – for the church week begins, like the Hebrew faith that formed it, in darkness and not in daylight – was also the start of the Jewish Festival of Lights, the holidays and the holy days of Hanukkah, which, spanning a sacred stretch of eight days in all, from the twenty-fifth of Kislev to the twenty-third of December, recalls each year the sectarian determination of the Maccabean partisans in the second century before the common era to resist the blandishments of Hellenistic culture and remain a consecrated people, the envoys of Yahweh, aloof and apart from the titillating Gentile civilisation that encircled them. Candle by ceremonial candle on the count of each cycle of twenty-four hours, menorahs will be lit in Israel and throughout the Dispersion to commemorate the rededication of the temple in Jerusalem, when the small supply of holy oil in its minute cruet burned eight times longer than its chemical life should have allowed it, as a sign of the presence of Providence, and the citadel of David was spared for a time its politic redeployment by a Seleucid potentate as an Aristotelian city-state, full of Greek ways and Greek weirdness. Christians of many persuasions and of none at all beyond the heartbreak of nostalgia for the safe house of their lost childhood continue the custom in another ecclesial calendar by placing electrical candelabra on their street-facing window sills through the Feast of Christmas and the Fast of January. Few may realise that they

213

have colonised a usage which itself cries out against cultural borrowing, that they have annexed an emblem which signifies, first and foremost, an absolute refusal to assimilate the alien.

The irony is, of course, reciprocal, as irony tends to be. For the celebration of Hanukkah, which happened traditionally as a rather minor matter in the rabbinic rotation of sacred time, has grown grandly, even grandiosely, in the space of two or three generations to become a cultural counterweight to the pagan and degraded Christmas of the post-religious states of the North world. Yet it has flourished most energetically in the United States where, in partnership with the low-church individualist Protestantism of the dominant ethos, American Jews have been assimilated and secularised beyond any historical precedent, European or otherwise, to the great grief of their more observant co-religionists and to the general loss of the religious disposition everywhere. For, if the twentieth century proved or, at any rate, posited anything, it was surely that morals without metaphysics, praxis without prayer, will be the extinction of our species; and that's not a spiritual slogan or a rallying cry for recruitment to the cause, but a simple sociological observation. To be sure, Christianity has disgraced itself often enough in the service of Christendom, and Judaism may yet do the same in the service of Zionism, for the political realisation of a religious ideal will always be a city of man and not of God; but an ethics that has abdicated the perspective of eternity, a witness that relinquishes worship, has already, in the supposed epoch of the Enlightenment, established a habit of moving from godless humanism to godforsaken inhumanity in a single, lethal lifetime.

Jew and Christian are at one in this understanding. Indeed, they're at one in almost everything. After all, they're not just cousins in the allegorical manner in which the evangelist Luke likes to represent the historical rapport between John the Baptist and Jesus of Nazareth in the early, eager decades of the first century, but brothers, siblings, twins even; in a sense Esau and Jacob, those two contending children of Rebecca, at the same time fractious and fraternal, as Columbia University historian Alan Segal's splendid simile suggests. In the twenty-third chapter of the Book of Beginnings, the Book of Genesis, God forewarns the matriarch who will mother Israel, 'Two nations are in thy womb, and two manner of people shall be separated from thy bowels'; and the citation serves as a signpost for Segal's subtle exegesis of the two revolutionary forms of monotheistic faith that survived the destruction of the Temple cult to re-group generously in its aftermath: on the one hand, the rabbinic academy with its meticulous Talmudic annotation of the Pentateuchal documents of the Covenant, and, on the other, the Jewish-Christian radicals with their rival reading of the martyric scriptures in the later prophetic volumes of the Hebrew Bible.

There's a handshake too, however fumbled, over the hairline fracture between the two dividing inheritors. The indications abound even in today's short gospel, where a tremendous, threefold interrogation, always a summons to ultimate seriousness, takes place as his ordinary petitioners inquire of the Baptist in three tart words, 'Ti ouv poiésómen?', 'What should we do?'; for the counsel that the desert father immediately gives them – 'He that has two coats, let him impart to him that has none' – will be repeated by his diligent disciple from Galilee three chapters later in Luke when Jesus commends, if not an identical donation, at least a comparable contribution, with his own invariable rider about non-retaliation, which emphasis is the peculiar preoccupation of the Lord throughout his ministry: 'And him that takes away your cloak forbid not to take your coat also'. In the same spirit, Luke will say of John at the Jordan that he evangelized the people, 'Evéngelizato ton laon', for the revivalist at the river is preaching the gospel of God and not just prefiguring it. Lucan as well is Saint Paul's untypical and perfect recollection in the Acts of the Apostles of the Baptist's famous disclaimer about the strap of the sandal he wasn't fit to unknot, for the former Pharisee is at least largely inattentive to the detail of Jesus' life; while, again, the whole of the third gospel will culminate in a chorus of praise and thanksgiving by the followers of Jesus in the precincts of a temple that has not yet been shed or superseded by an altered spirituality.

What has been set aside, however, by the thrust and tenor of the Jewish Christian initiative is particularity and apartness, the precise separatist energy that the holiday of Hanukkah salutes as the only rational antidote to eventual banality in a featureless and uniform world. Christianity is no Torah thoroughbred but a metropolitan mongrel which, by its own inherent double helix of adoption and adaptation, has roamed widely and wilfully among myths, metaphors and meanings, as if it were in a way the Creation's whirlwind curiosity about itself. It is protean where the other is purist, promiscuous where the other is chaste. In spite of the strict secular critique of its conduct over the centuries, it is deeply hospitable and not hostile to the biodiversity of culture. Indeed, it fetes the world and feasts upon it. But passion of this order always risks predation. Vigour can become violence, the love-act between faith and culture swerve from vows to violation. Are we consummating or consuming, or are we being consumed? At the end of the fourth century, the early Church adroitly appropriated the winter solstice shindig of the Roman imperial state as one among many strategic takeovers of pre-Christian territory, but the Feast of the Incarnation today has been tumbled by its own clever-dick tactics as the heightened holiday season silences the essential, dissenting, gravel-throated note of the fast within the feast.

This is not killjoy carping. Gaudete, which is the age-old name of the third Sunday in Advent and the customary Latin title of the medieval acclamation that opens this programme each week, calls a waiting people to the imperative of gaiety at a ghastly time: 'Let us rejoice!' Paul in Philippians is pitch-perfect:

'Chairete en Kyrió pantote. Palin eró chairete!' 'Rejoice in the Lord always! I repeat: Rejoice!' No wonder our Christmas hymns sound sometimes more like drinking songs, like the marvellous Methodist melodies you hear being belted out from the football terraces. They are, and ought to be, for the immensity of the meaning of the mystery of Bethlehem, to those who believe, cries out for a frenzy of foot-stamping and the flush of wine as much as for the rheumatic genuflections of the reverent elderly in the whispering transepts. For God's sake and for our sakes too there sounded a sort of hoarse barber's chorus over a zinc shed in a dormitory hamlet when an archangelic multitude roared out their Gloria to the shivering campesinos. Besides, as Sigmund Freud observed in the Viennese lectures which he delivered during the battle of the Somme, our relationship with the world is such that we cannot endure it uninterruptedly; and, belief or no belief in the newborn boy with breast milk on his lips, it is only right in this, the mortuary of the midwinter, that we should jig about under the heavenly host of the stars we have named and the stars we have numbered, if only to keep the foggy breath in our bodies. More a couch potato than a party animal, I know myself, through the lifelong gratifications of apathy, how much time must be wasted by each of us to make the rest worthwhile.

And yet; and yet. The rising of the solstice sun is not enough, since sunlight itself is absent from the scene in which a travelling god pitches his tarpaulin tent in a walled halting site among the settled people. Strong sunlight is too Greek for this strange, semitic venue. It's more a matter of moonlight or of moonshine even, according to the lurch of your own heart's leanings. Says the Second King in the late Ted Hughes' exquisite Nativity play, as he pauses before the sacking that serves as a shelter:

> He will be born to the coughing of animals
> Among the broken, rejected objects

In the corner that costs not a penny
In the darkness of the mouse and the spider.

Nativities galore will be performed this week across the Christian curve of the world, in parish churches with a poor acoustic and a worse public-address system, in cramped kindergarten classrooms with white blackboards and silver CCTV cameras, and in smelly assembly halls where the wooden horse has been recycled as the Holiday Inn with no vacancies; and, as always, the best seats in the front rows will be reserved for the visiting dignitaries, the Board of Governors, the Chair of the Parents' Conference, the Leadership Team in the parish office, the Bishop maybe if his P.A. ever rings back to confirm, while the mess will be cleaned up afterwards by women from Latvia, Mongolian mini-maids, Third-World wetbacks, the undocumented Maries of modernity, some of whom at least will be pregnant. For this is the true audacity of Christmas: that it belongs, finally and fundamentally, to those who are excluded from its celebration, which is why it cannot ever be wholly assimilated to the world's wherewithal. It is an answer to prayer that goes on to question both what we pray for and what we prey upon. It is, indeed, a question that begs another in the symmetry of a dear and double yearning. 'What do you seek?' says the Lord in the Gospel of John, as the two disciples of the Baptist quit their master's seminar for a more eccentric walkabout with Jesus; and they say to him in turn, 'Rabbi, where are you staying?'

Let us go and see.

Chapter Thirty-Six
SACRED COWS

A FEW SHORT YEARS AGO I was working as part of a three-person team on the broadcast of a Christmas service from a small Cistercian monastery somewhat outside the present cultural Pale but well within the historical terrain of that ancient Anglo-Norman enclave around the walled city of Dublin. Part of the paperwork for such events involves the payment of modest royalties to the composers of any copyright liturgical music to be used in the Mass: an entrance hymn, an alleluia, a memorial acclamation, a Great Amen; or, in the case of a parish folk group or a secondary school, say, something by Liam Lawton, John Lennon or the true Kapellmeister of our tormented era, Leonard Cohen, whose work of scriptural witness over forty years in the world comprises a modern psalter, a book of entreaty and bereavement, of gratefulness and humility, to stand beside the hundred and fifty psalms of the Hebrew Bible which is his birthright and his burden as a bare-headed Jew with a priestly surname. So I wrote a letter to the Abbot in Moone, Co. Kildare, asking for a list of the chants and the carols he intended to air; and, within a day or two, there was a letter from him in my in-tray.

Or was there? For, when I slit the package open with a pencil, its contents confused me. Instead of Glorias and doxologies, I was looking at a long column of old-fashioned female names – Molly, Victoria, Ellen, Goretti – and a precise, parallel ledger of these good ladies' average annual milk yields over a five-year period. I was momentarily perplexed. Perhaps there was something to be said, after all, for the Protestant dissolution of the monasteries. Perhaps they had been dissolute places. But I was only proving my credentials as a city boy whose nearness to nature never exceeded a certain respectful affection for a tortoise of indeterminate age and gender in the back garden of my childhood, upon whose patient shell I once initialled my three names in pink nail varnish taken from my mother's prohibited dressing table.

For I had forgotten that the Cistercians of the strict observance combine work and worship, liturgy and hard labour, devotion and dairy herds, in a radiant balance of the two worlds – spirit and sinew, chasubles and sileage –that the Feast of the Incarnation consecrates not as a double act or a two-tier duty but as one unified endeavour, the utter at-onement, in fact, of earth and air, time and eternity. One minute the monks might be writing a trilingual commentary on the Song of Songs, for the interpretation of that book of the Bible was, at a particular time in the history of the Order, almost a Cistercian monopoly; at another, they might be harvesting organic mushrooms or tackling a tractor's broken fan belt. And, right enough, on the other side of the recycled A4 paper pages, the Lord Abbot had scribbled a longhand Order of Service, complete with times and author's details, for the evening, a week later, of the transmission of the Eucharist from his community's chapel. Eco-sensitive as the Benedictine mentality always has been, since its earliest entry into agribusiness back in the Dark Ages when it supervised the reclamation of the aboriginal forests and the preservation of the Roman manor farm as a durable form for human survival, he was only trying to avoid waste, being, as the religious tend to be, a conserver – which is not to say a conservative. Conserving is the responsibility of radicals who operate as translators, the people of Pentecost, in the permanent dialogue between tradition and modernity.

If I go on about the dairy herd and the service details at a country Christmas Mass in the early millennium, it's not for the sake of the gag, but because of the great good news – the gospel truth, indeed – that a single scrap of paper brought me, with its prayers on one side and its prices on the other. If you held it up to the light, you could even see both scripts at the same time in a sort of seamless enmeshment, cows and canticles together. For the world is one and not two, let alone several. The economy that we like to practise – purity versus profanity, the sacred versus the secular, the holy versus the polluted – is a crafty human construct that equips us to do our expeditious business in a binary world; but it is not God's way. Leakage and linkage, mutuality amounting to unanimity, is how Providence has planned the one-flesh fulfilment of grace and nature; and the Nativity texts in the Jewish Gospel of Matthew and in the Greek Gospel of Luke profess this in their own rowdy and devout manner, though the detail is different because the two men are thinking and feeling in their own cultural vocabularies, just as you and I distinguish and discern in terms of our modern mythology, which is called empirical scientific rationality.

The semitic scenario in Matthew, full of Old Testament night terrors and turbulence, inserts the legend of the Magi not because it is true in terms of reportage (mere information is a minor matter in scripture) but because it is truthful, it is filled with truth about God's hospitality and our human hunger for it. The narrative of the Annunciation in the gentle, gentile imagination of Luke reverses the horrible copulatory maelstrom of sacred sex between mortal and immortal in much Mediterranean mythology of the age, to record instead the holy and whole-hearted reciprocity between a human agent and the immeasurable mystery we dare to identify in tiny, defiant words like 'God' and 'Lord' and 'Spirit'. And neither evangelist is denigrating ordinary intercourse, as sceptics allege, by referring Jesus' paternity to the God of Abraham instead of to the Joseph who is so often represented in literalist European iconography as a downcast cuckold outside the improvised canopy of Mary's child-bed in Behlehem, since Judaism, unlike its later Christian offspring, has always affirmed the creativity of the body to the point where the rabbis recommend the love-act as a Sabbath mitzvah or blessing. Instead, both Matthew and Luke are affirming that the life, death and risenness of Jesus of Nazareth, are not narrowly reducible to the sum of all the influences upon him, whether those of family, fatherland or faith itself, but that, above and beyond any biographical explanation, his presence among us as the very embodiment of God's word to the world, marks the benign intervention of divinity in the down-to-earth dailiness of our being. So the angelic choristers can harmonise their humming over a corrugated shelter while the short-legged insects in the bedding below grapple for a foothold in the slick and steaming afterbirth.

Twenty-five years ago I queued among large Wanted wall posters of bank robbers and kidnappers in a San Franciscan post office in order to propose to my Irish girlfriend by telegram, a stratagem I recommend to faint-hearted folk afraid of rejection in an expensive restaurant. She signalled acceptance in the same economy manner, counting her words according to her small change; and, several weeks later, I was on my way home to her for the holidays, as Americans choose to call Christmas for some curious, if courteous, multicultural reason. But I was stranded, a short-sleeved ex-pat, in a snowstorm in the international terminal at Heathrow Airport among many tall Christmas trees and no cribs at all. Every kind of person on the planet, from elongated Ethiopians to Aleutian Eskimos, from blonde backpackers in lumberjack shirts to Nigerian dignitaries in kaleidoscopic clothing, sat, slept, squabbled and spreadeagled on the hard seats around me in the shrill, squash-court acoustic of the walkways. Most used their baggage like sandbags to shore up aggressive impromptu cubicles made of cases, trolleys and crying children. At night silent elderly women in saris cleared away our cigarette butts and our sandwich wrappers smilingly, with broad brushes that made no sound as they swept in slow, stately circles. By day, I was down to tea bags and the last of the duty-free and more news on the public address about de-icers and the closure of the London tubeline while the snow continued to cascade down over the parked nosecones of the planes, over the petrified apron and the stiffened windsocks, like it was Holy Communion.

Then a man across from me stood up, shook out a rattan prayer mat among rucksacks and collapsible buggies and the plethora of the ordinary, found his bearings by some inner compass, turned towards the south of east, and began to pray the salat-al-maghreb, the Islamic prayer at sunset.

> Bismil laahir rahmaanir raheem
> Al hamdu lillahi rabbil aalameen!

> In the name of God, most gracious, most merciful
> Praise be to God, Lord of the Universe!

I had been meaning to visit the airport oratory, a soundproofed sanctuary with its noiseless orbiting camera lens and quiet carpeting, like a privy or an ATM. I had seen its arrowed signpost – a logo of the numeral two, like a figure genuflecting – near a stopped travolator. But this man of the Abrahamic family was surely right to bow, prostrate himself, and sit down in a public space in the midst of the people who are God's plenty, in the density of the visited earth. A Muslim had shown a Christian what a Christian, as a humanist of the Incarnation, should have known already: that the stench of a stable can be the odour of sanctity, that the beatific vision is no astronomer's striving but the actual stardust of our species, and that God's embrace of us, far from being the bland, benumbing bore that the secularists caricature as the chloroform of faith, infuses so much meaning into life that the pathos and the pain of it are often unendurable.

For my mother and my sisters were wrong to wait until the very last moment, at the west door of the church on a Sunday morning forty years ago, before they'd slip on their white mantillas for half-twelve Mass, just as Orthodox Jews are wrong to hang mezuzahs, metal canisters that contain verses from Deuteronomy, on every doorpost in their homes except the bathroom. Whether we exclude a parish car park or a private loo, there is no longer any godforsaken spot on the planet. The God of Abraham who is the Father of Jesus sends his spirit among us to hallow the here and now. 'It is both terrible and comforting to dwell in the inconceivable nearness of God,' wrote the Jesuit theologian Karl Rahner, 'but we have no choice. God is with us.'